MENTAL MATH
Computation Activities
for Anytime

by Richard S. Piccirilli, Ph.D.

SCHOLASTIC
PROFESSIONAL BOOKS

NEW YORK • TORONTO • LONDON • AUCKLAND • SYDNEY

*This book is dedicated to
the other three Pics plus two.*

Acknowledgments

No one writes a book alone. Helping me in the background are my wife, Fran, and my two daughters, Annette Marie and Marianne. They gave me the love and support to carry on. To my parents, Domenico and Frances, who have left their indelible mark on me, you taught me the meaning of hard work. To my many elementary students, graduate students, and teachers with whom I have worked over the past thirty years, I say thank you for your inspiration. To Doug Clements, who read an early manuscript, thanks for your advice and kind words. A special thank you to the ever-efficient Mark and Linda Decker who typed the manuscript.

RSP

Scholastic Inc. grants teachers permission to photocopy the reproducible patterns from this book for classroom use. No other part of this publication may be reproduced in whole or in part, or stored in a retrieval system, or transmitted in any form or by any means, electronic or mechanical, photocopying, recording, or otherwise, without written permission of the publisher. For information regarding permission, write to Scholastic Inc., 555 Broadway, New York, NY   10012-3999.

Designed by Jacqueline Swensen
Cover design by Vincent Ceci
Cover illustration by Tony DeLuna
Interior illustration by Ellen Joy Sasaki

ISBN 0-590-49796-0

12 11 10 9 8 7 6 5 4   *6 7 8 9/9*

Copyright © 1994 by Scholastic Inc.

Printed in U.S.A.

CONTENTS

Is mental computation an "extra"? No! The National Council of Teachers of Mathematics makes "number sense" a main goal of today's mathematics education. In an age of technology, mental computation is more important than before. What should be de-emphasized is paper-and-pencil computation. Mental computation is used alongside calculators, as a check to see if arithmetic problems that were entered are reasonable.

Richard Piccirilli has done all of us in mathematics education a service by presenting a clear, readable book on mental computation. Teachers will be able to integrate these activities into their curriculum throughout the year, which is just how these abilities should be developed. The activities are easy to understand and use. They will supplement any teacher's mathematics program. The strategies are not just "tricks" (although some are as fun as tricks!), but represent just that type of thinking real people use in real situations. You can't ask for more.

Douglas H. Clements, Professor
SUNY at Buffalo

INTRODUCTION

WHAT IS MENTAL COMPUTATION?

Mental computation is finding exact answers to computation examples and problems. All calculations are completed mentally without the use of pencil and paper, calculator or other recording devices. In the process, the mind is not used as a blackboard in the sense that when adding 18+9, you think 8+9 is 17, put down the seven and carry the one. Rather, mental computation is a creative thinking process that requires the individual to invent procedures to deal with the unique computation example at hand.

We need to be reminded that not all examples can be done mentally. Only a subset of examples can be answered through mental computation. However, which examples can or cannot be done mentally more often than not will depend on the skill level of the user.

WHY IS MENTAL COMPUTATION IMPORTANT TO TEACH?

Mental computation is important because it is a **useful skill**. Very often, we can deal with many number situations in easy, quick, efficient, and exact ways. Mental computation is inexpensive in terms of cost, time, energy, memory load, and fatigue. Often it is the only tool we can use when there is a need for an immediate and exact answer.

More mathematics textbook series have incorporated a Mental Math component into their books. They have followed the lead of the National Council of Teachers of Mathematics. The Curriculum and Evaluation Standards For School Mathematics published by National Council of Teachers of Mathematics has stated that students should be able to "...select and use an appropriate method for computing from among mental arithmetic, pencil-and-paper, calculator, and computer methods." They further recognize the contribution mental computation can make toward understanding and reinforcing the regular math curriculum. The mathematics teacher's day is filled with trying to teach number properties, refinement of estimates, understanding place value, math operations, and problem solving, all while trying to make math meaningful. So, why is mental computation important to teach? It is important to teach because it contributes greatly to the rest of the math curriculum. Also, I cannot begin to mention what it does for student attitude and achievement.

WHAT IS THE BEST WAY TO USE THIS BOOK?

There is no one best way to use this book. Both a systematic and a random plan may be used. Common sense and having fun are important guides in the use of this book. Ultimately you should work out your own plan. Pick and choose activities appropriate for your level. You need the time and experience to build your own arsenal of mental computation strategies. You also need the freedom to vary your lessons. This book's approach is suggestive rather than prescriptive.

For those wishing a systematic or sequential plan to mental computation, start with activities that contribute to or are directly related to whole number operations. Start with addition and continue with subtraction, multiplication, and division. I would suggest starting with the very easy activities regardless of the grade you teach since it will help guarantee quick success and lay the foundation for the more advanced topics of fractions, decimals, percents, and exponents.

Consistent with a systematic or sequential plan is teaching the **FOUR BASIC STRATE-GIES**. You may want your students to memorize these four strategies and see and learn about them directly. Further, you may want to bring the four basic strategies out in discussions during the course of teaching the various lessons.

A random plan to mental computation suggests that you get your feet wet first. The order of mental computation topics is of less importance than exploring, sharing ideas, seeing what the class can do, doing number tricks, and having fun. Do the very easy activities and then pick and choose what suits your current interests or area of the curriculum. A random plan easily can lead to a systematic yet flexible approach to mental computation.

Each plan can have elements of the other. Do what feels right for you and your students. Don't commit yourself to an approach yet. If you vacillate between approaches, be assured that your students are still learning a great number of mental computation techniques and strategies. As you continue to use this book, you will begin to work out your own approach. And do you know what? That's good!

The following suggestions should serve as a guide to enable you to maximize your time and energy to teach mental computation:

1. Become familiar with what you will be teaching. It will help you to prepare more meaningful and fun lessons.

2. Spend the necessary time to preteach and do oral work before assigning student activity pages. Give students opportunities to invent or predict what strategies are to come. I've indicated with a logo those pages you may want to make into overhead transparencies.

3. Have students discuss their own thinking with the class. This is where students share their invented strategies and develop readiness.

4. Be flexible. Modify any lesson or pupil activity sheet to suit special needs.

5. Use the Warm-Ups. They can quickly build confidence. Be sure to use the pages that help to point out the usefulness of mental computation.

6. Have fun with the mental computation strategies. Mystify your students and encourage them to teach the strategies to friends or family members.

7. Use about ten minutes of class time three times per week. It will help to keep newly developed strategies alive.

8. Show your class examples that best pertain to their level of understanding. You don't need to do all the sections of an activity. Where there is a wide range of grades 4 - 8 ideas, pick and choose what will work best for your class.

There are **four basic strategies** for doing mental computation.

> *** DECOMPOSE NUMBERS**
>
> *** MAKE EASY NUMBERS**
>
> *** SUBSTITUTE AN EQUAL NUMBER**
>
> *** COMPENSATE**

Mental computation may employ one strategy or a combination of these strategies. It is important that students become familiar with the basic strategies. Teachers have shown overhead transparencies of the examples under each strategy without discussing the strategy. For instance, they asked students how they would mentally arrive at the answer for 64 + 25, under the first strategy, breaking the number apart. After shared thinking, the students showed their solutions. This continued in short sessions with all of the examples under the four basic strategies. Surprisingly, the students found that the strategy on the overhead transparency agreed with their own thinking! Also, teachers were surprised to see other creative solutions their students invented.

I encourage you to help your students make the link between the four basic strategies and the mental computation strategies they will encounter and/or invent. The heart of this section is to allow students to DISCUSS the strategies. Teachers and students need to use these strategies constantly and in creative ways as they work through the lesson. Always ask, "What strategy are you using?"

Pages 8–10 give examples of each strategy used either by itself or in combination with other strategies.

MENTAL COMPUTATION—BASIC STRATEGY

DECOMPOSE NUMBERS

To **decompose** you break apart numbers into meaningful and useful units or groups that can be easily recomposed.

ADDITION:

64 + 25	28 + 59
64 + 20 + 5	(20 + 8) + (50 + 9)
84 + 5	(20 + 50) + (8 + 9)
89	70 + 17
	87

SUBTRACTION:

87 - 13	130 - 84	125 - 60
87 - 10 - 3	130 - 80 - 4	120 - 60 + 5
77 - 3	50 - 4	60 + 5
74	46	65

127 - 38	105 - 9	2,800 - 1,200
127 - 30 - 8	105 - 5 - 4	**Think:** 28 - 12
97 - 8	100 - 4	16
89	96	2,800 - 1,200
		1,600

MULTIPLICATION:

3 x 48	20 x 34	102 x 35
(3 x 40) + (3 x 8)	(2 x 10) x 34	(100 + 2) x 35
120 + 24	(2 x 34) x 10	3,500 + 70
144	68 x 10	3,570
	680	

60 x 30		6 x 3
(6 x 10) x (3 x 10)	**Or**	then attach
(6 x 3) x (10 x 10)		two zeros
18 x 100		1,800
1,800		

DIVISION:

42 ÷ 3	396 ÷ 4	416 ÷ 8
(30 + 12) ÷ 3	(400 - 4) ÷ 4	(400 + 16) ÷ 8
10 + 4	100 - 1	50 + 2
14	99	52

MENTAL COMPUTATION—BASIC STRATEGY

MAKE EASY NUMBERS

To **make easy numbers** you put numbers together that are simple to use. This usually involves changing the order of numbers.

Examples of numbers which are easy to compute:

20 + 30	90 - 60	86 x 10	270 ÷ 90
50	30	860	3

Maneuvering to **make easy numbers**:

4 + 87 + 6	23 + 14 + 5 + 6	97 - 12
(4 + 6) + 87	14 + 6 + 23 + 5	(97 - 10) - 2
10 + 87	20 + 23 + 5	87 - 2
97	43 + 5	85
	48	

36 x 5 x 2	7 x 50 x 7 x 2	4 x 7 x 25 x 6
36 x 10	(7 x 7) x (2 x 50)	(4 x 25) x (7 x 6)
360	49 x 100	100 x 42
	4,900	4,200

$\frac{1}{6}$ x 13 x 18

($\frac{1}{6}$ x 18) x 13

3 x 13

3 x (10 + 3)   (decomposing)

30 + 9

39

25 x 36

($\frac{1}{4}$ x 100) x 36

$\frac{1}{4}$ x (100 x 36)

$\frac{1}{4}$ x 3,600

900

MENTAL COMPUTATION—BASIC STRATEGY

SUBSTITUTE AN EQUAL NUMBER

To **substitute** you replace a value with another equal value that is easier to manipulate.

$\frac{1}{6}$ x 420

420 ÷ 6   (substituting a whole

70   number for a fraction)

50% of 60

$\frac{1}{2}$ x 60   (substituting a

30   fraction for a percent)

or

60 ÷ 2

30

.75 x 24

$\frac{3}{4}$ x 24   (substituting a fraction

for a decimal)

(24 ÷ 4) x 3

6 x 3

18

624 x 5

(624 x 10) ÷ 2   (rename 5 as 10÷ 2)

6,240 ÷ 2

3,120

COMPENSATE

*To **compensate** you may work in two ways: a number is changed and then the answer is adjusted, or both numbers are adjusted so there is no need to change the answer.*

ADJUSTING THE ANSWER	ADJUSTING THE NUMBERS

ADJUSTING THE ANSWER

$$43 + 39$$
$$43 + (40 - 1)$$
$$83 - 1$$
$$82$$

ADJUSTING THE NUMBERS

$$43 \rightarrow 42$$
$$+ 39 \rightarrow + 40$$
$$82 \qquad 82$$

Lower the 43 by **1**.
Raise the 40 by **1**.

$$276 + 98$$
$$276 + (100 - 2)$$
$$376 - 2$$
$$374$$

$$276 \rightarrow 274$$
$$+ 98 \rightarrow + 100$$
$$374 \qquad 374$$

Lower the 276 by **2**.
Raise the 98 by **2**.

$$276 - 98$$
$$276 (- 98 - 2) + 2$$
Note: Subtract 2 more then
add 2 more to the answer
$$276 - 100 (+ 2)$$
$$176 + 2$$
$$178$$

$$276 \rightarrow 278$$
$$- 98 \rightarrow -100$$
$$178 \qquad 178$$

Raise both numbers by **2**.

$$6\tfrac{5}{8} + 3\tfrac{7}{8}$$
$$6\tfrac{5}{8} + (4 - \tfrac{1}{8})$$
$$10\tfrac{5}{8} - \tfrac{1}{8}$$
$$10\tfrac{4}{8} = 10\tfrac{1}{2}$$

$$6\tfrac{5}{8} + 3\tfrac{7}{8}$$
$$6\tfrac{4}{8} + 3\tfrac{8}{8}$$
$$6\tfrac{4}{8} + 4$$
$$10\tfrac{4}{8} = 10\tfrac{1}{2}$$

Lower $6\tfrac{5}{8}$ by $\tfrac{1}{8}$.
Raise $3\tfrac{7}{8}$ by $\tfrac{1}{8}$.

These Warm-Ups can help you and your students break into *mental computation*. You can be flexible and use what you like or what may be appropriate for the level of your class.

The purposes of Warm-Ups are:

* to begin discussing strategies
* to value mental computation
* to strengthen visualization of numbers
* to build teacher and student confidence
* to strengthen some basic math skills
* to have fun with recreational math.

Use **A CLASS CHALLENGE** and **SAVING TIME** to help students see and appreciate the power of mental computation. With **A CLASS CHALLENGE**, be sure that you study how the examples are done mentally. Feel free to design your own examples to add to what is already there or to reflect what your class can handle. There are plenty of other examples throughout this book that you can include in your **CLASS CHALLENGE**. To use **SAVING TIME**, make an overhead transparency and have pupils discuss how each example could have been done mentally.

Using **THOSE EVERYDAY SITUATIONS** could begin with a class discussion of situations or problems that have required students to find a mental solution. You may want to defer finding all the answers to a time when the class has had more experience with mental computation.

Many of the remaining Warm-Ups can be used as worksheets or in combination with an overhead transparency. You can use the transparency to get students started on the mental activity. The next step is to ask students how they arrived at answers. Discuss strategies. Let pupils share their thinking. This is when other pupils start to pick up new strategies they haven't thought about. Again, shared thinking is the heart of all lessons in mental computation. After discussing strategies, students should complete the remaining portion of the worksheet.

The **PHOTOGRAPHIC MEMORY** activities and **THINKING ABOUT DATES** are motivational, fun activities. Make transparencies so everyone can see the numbers as each activity is presented. When you are ready to explain the activities, reproduce the activity sheets. Some teachers have used these activities as teasers, or until someone has figured out how the "tricks" are done. (See the answer key for answers to all problems.)

A Class Challenge

° °

To help students appreciate the power of mental computation, challenge them to a contest. Choose some or all of the examples provided below. Duplicate and cut out the boxes. Fold them and put them in a coffee cup or some similar container. Like a magician, *be sure to practice the skills first!* The pages you need to study are listed below. Use only those that are appropriate for your students' level. You may want to add others from different sections of the book.

SAY: I'd like to challenge the class to a contest. I will let you use paper/pencil or a calculator to come up with answers to math examples that I have in a coffee cup. I will only use my head, and I think that I can beat you every time by coming up with the correct answer first.

PROCEDURE:

* Select four students. Each will be a selector, recorder, starter, and judge respectively.
* The first student will select at random a folded example from the cup.
* The second student will record the example on the board while you and the challengers turn away from the board.
* The third student will say GO so that you and your challengers see the example and start at the same time.
* The fourth student will judge who finishes first.
* Write your answer on the board, while students shout out the answer.

EXAMPLES:

1. From 10,000 take away 3,642 =

$1,000,000 − $268,783 = **[Page 36]**

2. 24,342 x 11 = **[Page 38]**

5 x 86,428 = **[Page 40]**

3. 50 x 428 =

268 x 500 = **[Page 40]**

4. 4 x 300 x 25 =

2 x 4 x 25 x 50 = **[Page 39]**

5. 35^2 =

95^2 = **[Page 86]**

6. 9 x 999 =

7 x 9,999 = **[Page 41]**

7. $3.50 \div \frac{1}{4}$ = **[Page 63]**

.0167 ÷ 100 = **[Page 76]**

8. $\sqrt{7,225}$ =

$\sqrt{3,025}$ = **[Page 86]**

9. $\frac{12}{N} = \frac{48}{60}$

$\frac{8}{9} = \frac{32}{N}$ **[Page 60]**

10 150% of 60 = **[Page 80]**

18% of 50 = **[Page 82]**

Saving Time

How could these examples have been done *mentally* **without** the use of pencil-and-paper, calculator, or computer?

1.
$$
\begin{array}{r}
6\overset{4}{\cancel{5}}\overset{1}{0} \\
-649 \\
\hline
001
\end{array}
$$

2.
$$
\begin{array}{r}
392 \\
+101 \\
\hline
493
\end{array}
$$

3.
$$
\begin{array}{r}
\overset{1\ 1}{\$5.99} \\
+2.86 \\
\hline
\$8.85
\end{array}
$$

4.
$$
\begin{array}{r}
\overset{1}{75} \\
50 \\
+25 \\
\hline
150
\end{array}
$$

5.
$$
\begin{array}{r}
\overset{2\ 1}{\$1.95} \\
1.95 \\
+1.95 \\
\hline
\$5.85
\end{array}
$$

6.
$$
\begin{array}{r}
47 \\
\times 10 \\
\hline
00 \\
47 \\
\hline
470
\end{array}
$$

7.
$$
\begin{array}{r}
125 \\
\times 100 \\
\hline
000 \\
000 \\
125 \\
\hline
12{,}500
\end{array}
$$

8.
$$
\begin{array}{r}
1\frac{3}{4} = 1\frac{3}{4} \\
2\frac{1}{2} = 2\frac{2}{4} \\
+1\frac{1}{4} = 1\frac{1}{4} \\
\hline
4\frac{6}{4} = 4 + 1\frac{2}{4} = 5\frac{2}{4} = 5\frac{1}{2}
\end{array}
$$

9.
$$
\begin{array}{r}
4 = 3\frac{5}{5} \\
-1\frac{3}{5} = 1\frac{3}{5} \\
\hline
2\frac{2}{5}
\end{array}
$$

10. $4\frac{4}{8} \div \frac{1}{2} =$
$\frac{36}{8} \div \frac{1}{2} =$
$\frac{36}{8} \times \frac{2}{1} = \frac{72}{8} = 9$

11. $1\frac{3}{4} \times 12 =$
$\frac{7}{4} \times \frac{12}{1} = \frac{84}{4} = 21$

12.
$$
\begin{array}{r}
32 \\
\times .50 \\
\hline
00 \\
160 \\
\hline
16.00
\end{array}
$$

13.
$$
\begin{array}{r}
.006 \\
\times .004 \\
\hline
024 \\
000 \\
000 \\
\hline
.000024
\end{array}
$$

14. $2 - 1.75 =$
$$
\begin{array}{r}
\overset{1}{\overset{1}{\cancel{2}}}\overset{9}{.}\overset{1}{0}0 \\
-1.75 \\
\hline
0.25
\end{array}
$$

15. $33\frac{1}{3}\% \times 18 =$
$$
\begin{array}{r}
18 \\
\times .33\frac{1}{3} \\
\hline
6 \\
54 \\
54 \\
\hline
6.00
\end{array}
$$

Those Everyday Situations

Can you come up with an exact answer to the following situations? Since you weren't expecting to encounter these situations, you have no pencil/paper or calculator. (Assume no sales tax.) Write the answer in the space provided.

1. You are traveling from your home to Rochester, New York. The highway sign says "Rochester 500 mi." You have traveled 268 miles already. How far is Rochester from where you live?

_____

2. You cut lawns for $10.00 per lawn. How many lawns will you need to cut to afford a $120.00 bicycle?

_____

3. The recipe calls for 3/4 cup of peanut butter. How much do you need if you double the recipe?

_____

4. You are taking a math test. You have pencil and paper with you. You are running out of time. How can you quickly answer 6 x 7.98?

_____

5. You are treating yourself and a friend to a movie. Tickets are $4.50 each. How much money will you have left from $10.00 to buy popcorn?

_____

6. Twenty-four people will be at the birthday party. How many bags of potato chips are needed? A bag of potato chips serves 8 people.

_____

7. You answer a trivia question from a radio station contest and win 400 nickels. How much money did you win?

_____

8. Which is the best deal on CD's? 2/$12.00, or 3/$18.00, or 4/$23.00?

_____

Name _____

After Numbers

○ ○

Find the answer. Use mental computation. Write your answers below.

1. What number comes

    after 12? _____

    after 99? _____

    after 22? _____

    after 100? _____

    after 999? _____

2. What number comes

    2 **after** 16? _____

    2 **after** 31? _____

    2 **after** 93? _____

    2 **after** 99? _____

    2 **after** 111? _____

3. What number comes

    10 **after** 23? _____

    10 **after** 96? _____

    10 **after** 112? _____

    10 **after** 214? _____

    10 **after** 396? _____

4. What number comes

    9 **after** 27? _____

    9 **after** 43? _____

    9 **after** 58? _____

    9 **after** 93? _____

    9 **after** 116? _____

    9 **after** 207? _____

    9 **after** 438? _____

    9 **after** 679? _____

5. What number comes

    11 **after** 86? _____

    11 **after** 29? _____

    11 **after** 91? _____

    11 **after** 157? _____

    11 **after** 245? _____

6. What number comes

    100 **after** 21? _____

    100 **after** 236? _____

    100 **after** 746? _____

    100 **after** 923? _____

    100 **after** 764? _____

7. What number comes

    101 **after** 37? _____

    101 **after** 289? _____

    101 **after** 871? _____

    101 **after** 723? _____

    101 **after** 2,342? _____

8. What number comes

    99 **after** 35? _____

    99 **after** 168? _____

    99 **after** 273? _____

    99 **after** 198? _____

    99 **after** 456? _____

    99 **after** 499? _____

    99 **after** 533? _____

    99 **after** 786? _____

Can you make up any of your own problem using 1,000; 1,001; or 999?

Name ______________________________

Skip Counting

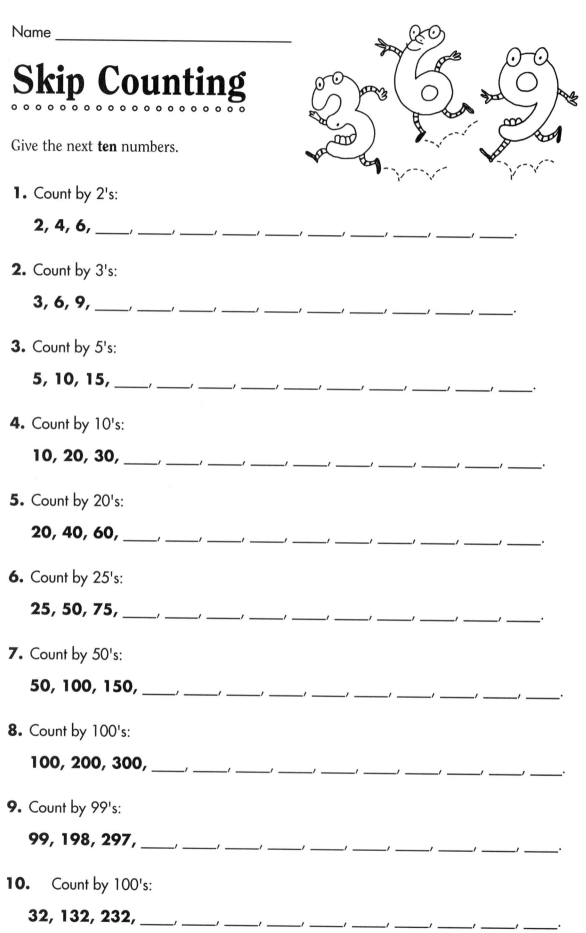

Give the next **ten** numbers.

1. Count by 2's:

2, 4, 6, ____, ____, ____, ____, ____, ____, ____, ____, ____, ____.

2. Count by 3's:

3, 6, 9, ____, ____, ____, ____, ____, ____, ____, ____, ____, ____.

3. Count by 5's:

5, 10, 15, ____, ____, ____, ____, ____, ____, ____, ____, ____, ____.

4. Count by 10's:

10, 20, 30, ____, ____, ____, ____, ____, ____, ____, ____, ____, ____.

5. Count by 20's:

20, 40, 60, ____, ____, ____, ____, ____, ____, ____, ____, ____, ____.

6. Count by 25's:

25, 50, 75, ____, ____, ____, ____, ____, ____, ____, ____, ____, ____.

7. Count by 50's:

50, 100, 150, ____, ____, ____, ____, ____, ____, ____, ____, ____, ____.

8. Count by 100's:

100, 200, 300, ____, ____, ____, ____, ____, ____, ____, ____, ____, ____.

9. Count by 99's:

99, 198, 297, ____, ____, ____, ____, ____, ____, ____, ____, ____, ____.

10. Count by 100's:

32, 132, 232, ____, ____, ____, ____, ____, ____, ____, ____, ____, ____.

Name _____

Before Numbers

○ ○

Find the answer. Use mental computation. Write your answers in the space provided.

1. What number comes

    before 7? _____

    before 100? _____

    before 201? _____

    before 550? _____

    before 777? _____

2. What number comes

    3 **before** 993? _____

    3 **before** 200? _____

    3 **before** 301? _____

    3 **before** 557? _____

    3 **before** 641? _____

3. What number comes

    10 **before** 33? _____

    10 **before** 241? _____

    10 **before** 516? _____

    10 **before** 808? _____

    10 **before** 1,000? _____

4. What number comes

    9 **before** 87? _____

    9 **before** 24? _____

    9 **before** 31? _____

    9 **before** 40? _____

    9 **before** 98? _____

5. What number comes

    100 **before** 382? _____

    100 **before** 491? _____

    100 **before** 705? _____

    100 **before** 999? _____

    100 **before** 1,111? _____

6. What number comes

    5 **before** 19? _____

    5 **before** 36? _____

    5 **before** 57? _____

    5 **before** 71? _____

    5 **before** 99? _____

7. What number comes

    99 **before** 367? _____

    99 **before** 500? _____

    99 **before** 428? _____

    99 **before** 362? _____

    99 **before** 145? _____

8. What number comes

    4 **before** 67? _____

    4 **before** 105? _____

    4 **before** 99? _____

    4 **before** 528? _____

    4 **before** 300? _____

Name _____

Skipping Backward

○ ○

Count backwards. Give the next **ten** numbers.

1. Count by 2's:

90, 88, 86, ____, ____, ____, ____, ____, ____, ____, ____, ____, ____.

2. Count by 3's:

60, 57, 54, ____, ____, ____, ____, ____, ____, ____, ____, ____, ____.

3. Count by 5's:

120, 115, 110, ____, ____, ____, ____, ____, ____, ____, ____, ____, ____.

4. Count by 10's:

170, 160, 150, ____, ____, ____, ____, ____, ____, ____, ____, ____, ____.

5. Count by 20's:

400, 380, 360, ____, ____, ____, ____, ____, ____, ____, ____, ____, ____.

6. Count by 25's:

325, 300, 275, ____, ____, ____, ____, ____, ____, ____, ____, ____, ____.

7. Count by 50's:

800, 750, 700, ____, ____, ____, ____, ____, ____, ____, ____, ____, ____.

8. Count by 100's:

2,000; 1,900; 1,800; _____; _____; _____; _____; _____; _____; _____;

_____; _____; _____.

9. Count by 99's:

1,287; 1,188; 1,089; _____; _____; _____; _____; _____; _____; _____;

_____; _____; _____.

10. Count by 10's:

343, 333, 323, ____, ____, ____, ____, ____, ____, ____, ____, ____, ____.

18

One Hundred Chart

Reproduce the chart below on a transparency. Let students study it for one minute.

1	2	3	4	5	6	7	8	9	10
11	12	13	14	15	16	17	18	19	20
21	22	23	24	25	26	27	28	29	30
31	32	33	34	35	36	37	38	39	40
41	42	43	44	45	46	47	48	49	50
51	52	53	54	55	56	57	58	59	60
61	62	63	64	65	66	67	68	69	70
71	72	73	74	75	76	77	78	79	80
81	82	83	84	85	86	87	88	89	90
91	92	93	94	95	96	97	98	99	100

Name _____

Easy Figuring
○ ○

Think about the **One Hundred Chart**. Name the rest of the numbers in each column.

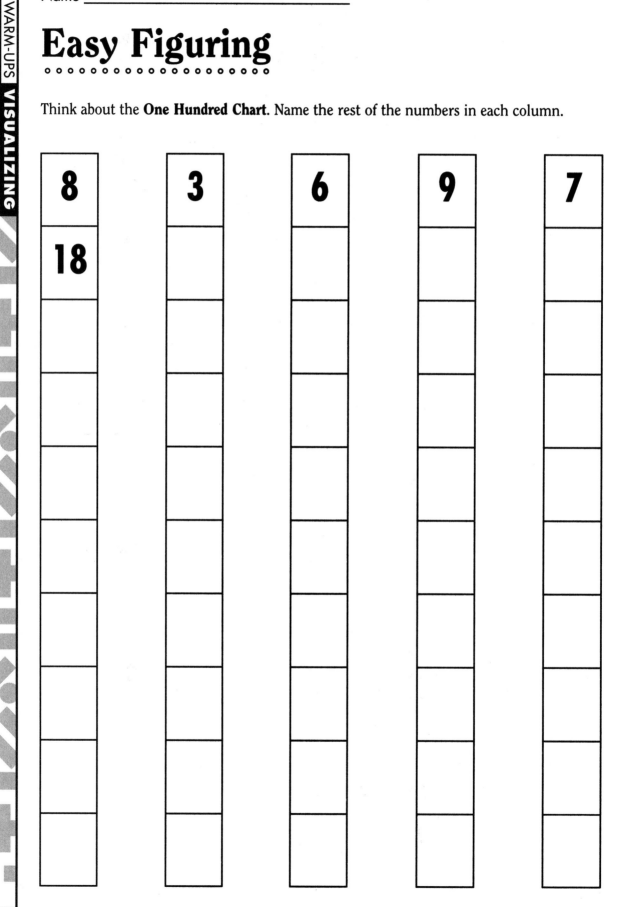

8	3	6	9	7
18				

Name _____

Find the Secret Number

Break the code to discover the secret number. The code uses the symbols ↑, ↓, ←, →
and the **One Hundred Chart**. Study the **One Hundred Chart** for one minute.

1. What number is one above 46 (↑) ? _____

2. What number is three below 25 (↓↓↓) ? _____

3. What number is three to the left and one above 50 (←←←↑) ? _____

4. What number is 33 ↑ → → (read as 33, up one space,

and two spaces to the right)? _____

5. 72 ↑↑→ ? _____

6. 16 ↓↓↓← ? _____

7. 85 ↓→→ ? _____

8. 28 ←←↑←↓ ? _____

9. 33 ↑↑→→ ? _____

10. 12 ↓↓↓←← ? _____

11. 45 ↑↑→↓→ ? _____

12. 100 ↑↑←← ? _____

13. 1 →→↓↓↓↓ ? _____

14. 38 ↑↑←←←↓ ? _____

15. 74 →↓↓→→→ ? _____

16. 50 ↑↑→→↑← ? _____

17. 4 ↓↓↓→ ? _____

18. 16 ↓↓→→↓← ? _____

19. 30 ↑←←↓↓ ? _____

20. 23 ↑↑→→↓↓← ? _____

Now look back at the **One Hundred Chart**. Did you break the codes ?

Name _____

What's in the box?

○ ○

Remember the **One Hundred Chart**? Place the missing diagonal numbers in the boxes below.

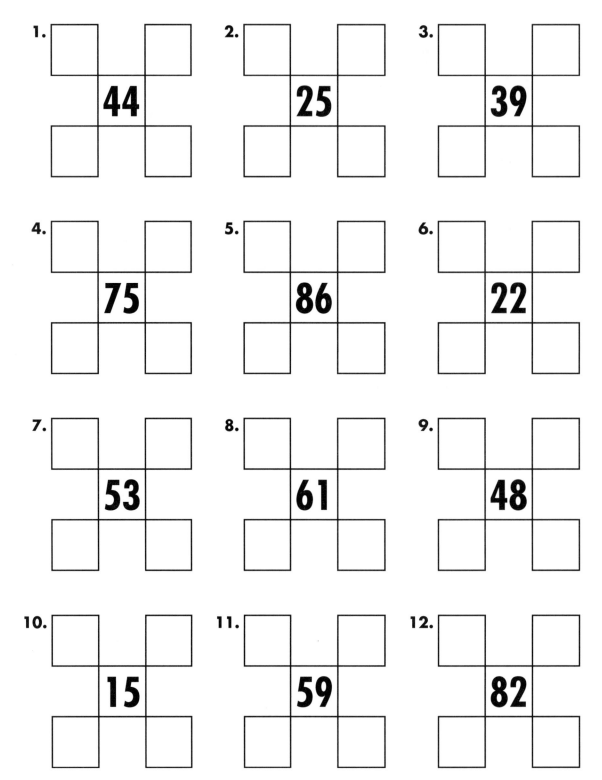

Photographic Memory for the Professional and the Amateur
SECRET SWISS SAVINGS ACCOUNT NUMBERS

o o o o o o o o o o o o o o o o o o o o o o o o o o o o o o o o o o o

DIRECTIONS: Make an overhead transparency of the Account Numbers on page 24. Have a volunteer point to any Passbook Number. Then, while not looking, you either recite or write the Account Number on the board.

FOR THE AMATEUR:

Passbook 15 is chosen.

Step 1: Add 12 to the Passbook Number. $15 + 12 = 27$

Step 2: Reverse the order of the digits.
These are the first digits in the Account Number. $27 \rightarrow$ **72**

Step 3: Add these two digits to get the third digit. $7 + 2 = 9 \rightarrow$ **729**

Step 4: In cases when the sum of the digits is 10 or greater, the tens digit is dropped, and the ones digit is kept.

FOR THE PROFESSIONAL:

Passbook 26 is chosen.

Step 1: Add 13 to the Passbook number. $26 + 13 = 39$

Step 2: Reverse the digits. $39 \rightarrow$ **93**

Step 3: Next, add those two digits together. If the sum of the two digits is a two-digit number, retain the digit in the ones place and discard the tens digit. This becomes your third digit.

$9 + 3 = 12$ (Drop the 1. 2 is your third digit.) $\rightarrow$ **932**

Step 4: Add the last two digits to get the fourth digit. $3 + 2 = 5 \rightarrow$ **9325**

Step 5: Add the last two digits. $2 + 5 = 7 \rightarrow$ **93257**

Then add $5 + 7$. $5 + 7 = 12$. (Drop the tens digit.) $\rightarrow$ **932572**

Continue in this manner until nine digits are reached

To find a Passbook Number, have a student give the Savings Account Number. After all the digits are given, you need to deal with the first two digits only. Take the first two digits, reverse them, and then subtract 12. For the Professional, you would follow the same procedure but subtract 13.

Individual students or a cooperative team of students can make up their own series of numbers. Encourage them to start with fewer than 9 digits in the Account Number, and to use fewer than 20 Passbook Numbers.

Photographic Memory
SECRET SWISS SAVINGS ACCOUNT NUMBERS

So, you think you have a good memory? Try mine. Below are 40 Passbook Numbers. Each has a secret account number. Let me study the sheet for 10 seconds. Then you may ask me the **Secret Swiss Savings Account Number** for any Passbook Number.

FOR THE AMATEUR

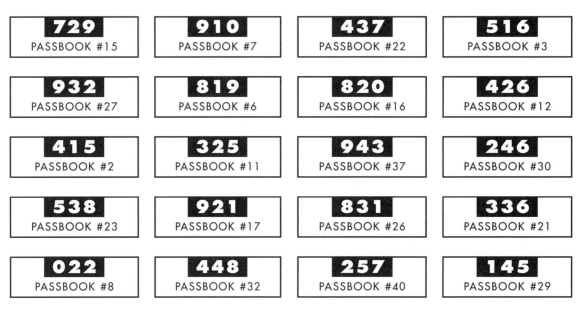

729 PASSBOOK #15	**910** PASSBOOK #7	**437** PASSBOOK #22	**516** PASSBOOK #3
932 PASSBOOK #27	**819** PASSBOOK #6	**820** PASSBOOK #16	**426** PASSBOOK #12
415 PASSBOOK #2	**325** PASSBOOK #11	**943** PASSBOOK #37	**246** PASSBOOK #30
538 PASSBOOK #23	**921** PASSBOOK #17	**831** PASSBOOK #26	**336** PASSBOOK #21
022 PASSBOOK #8	**448** PASSBOOK #32	**257** PASSBOOK #40	**145** PASSBOOK #29

FOR THE PROFESSIONAL

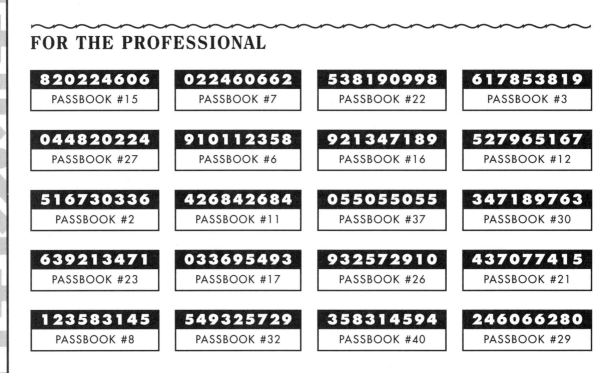

820224606 PASSBOOK #15	**022460662** PASSBOOK #7	**538190998** PASSBOOK #22	**617853819** PASSBOOK #3
044820224 PASSBOOK #27	**910112358** PASSBOOK #6	**921347189** PASSBOOK #16	**527965167** PASSBOOK #12
516730336 PASSBOOK #2	**426842684** PASSBOOK #11	**055055055** PASSBOOK #37	**347189763** PASSBOOK #30
639213471 PASSBOOK #23	**033695493** PASSBOOK #17	**932572910** PASSBOOK #26	**437077415** PASSBOOK #21
123583145 PASSBOOK #8	**549325729** PASSBOOK #32	**358314594** PASSBOOK #40	**246066280** PASSBOOK #29

Follow Me

+ - × ÷

5	6	7	8	9
0	1	2	3	4

DIRECTIONS: Reproduce the above chart on a chart or a transparency and show it to your class.

* Say "Follow Me."
* Point to the 2.
* Point to the x.
* Point to the 8.
* Ask, "What's the answer?"

Below are some examples you can use to get the game going. Be sure to point slowly to each number and operation symbol.

6 x 5	9 x 7	4 x 9 ÷ 6
3 + 5	9 - 4 x 5	2 + 3 x 2 x 6
8 + 1 x 2	3 x 4 + 2	5 x 9 ÷ 5
4 x 6	2 x 2 x 2 x 2	7 - 0 + 3 x 0 + 9
8 ÷ 2 + 1	5 x 2 x 9	6 ÷ 3 + 2 x 5
3 + 4 + 2	4 x 5 ÷ 2 + 3	5 - 3 - 1 x 6 x 3
4 x 4 + 4	8 ÷ 1 x 8	7 - 4 x 3 x 3

* You can do uneven division so that fractions are part of the **Follow Me** game. Try 3 ÷ 2 + 4.

* You can drill number facts. Try 3 x 6, 8 x 6, 5 x 6, and so on.

* To assist with the carrying step in multiplication, you may want to include an addition step. Try 3 x 6 + 2, 8 x 6 + 5, 5 x 6 + 7, and so on.

* Let pupils make up their own examples and try them before the class. Be sure they know the answers ahead of time.

Thinking About Dates

Have students select three consecutive numbers on a calendar without telling you what they are. Ask for the sum of the dates. Take the answer and divide by 3. (You have just found the average of the three numbers which is the middle number of the three dates.) Note that all sums will be divisible by 3. The number before and the number after the average are the other two numbers.

> **EXAMPLE:** The dates are 22, 23, 24.
> The sum is 69.
> Divide 69 by 3. $69 \div 3 = 23$
> The number before 23 is 22.
> The number after 23 is 24.
> The dates are 22, 23, 24.

SUGGESTIONS

Embellish the trick by putting your hand on the calendar. Say you are getting vibrations from the calendar and say, "I see a 22. Yes, I see a 22, 23, and 24."

VARIATIONS

* Three numbers in a column also may be chosen. Ask for the sum. Find the average. Then subtract and add 7 to the average to get the smallest and largest numbers respectively.

* Have students choose a 3 x 3 square of numbers. Say you will tell them all the numbers in the square.

  • Ask them to tell you the total of any row or column and to tell you which row or column they've chosen.

  • Once the average is found, you find the other numbers for the row. The column tells you which of the three digits in the second row is known. From this you calculate all others.

  • Then find the numbers for the remaining rows using the methods from three numbers in a row and using the method from three numbers in a column.

* The same procedure can be used with three consecutive numbers from 1-100.

* To add three consecutive numbers mentally, multiply the second number by 3. As a check, the sum of the digits in the answer must be divisible by 3.

USING MENTAL COMPUTATION WITH WHOLE NUMBERS

Hold class discussions prior to the assignment of any worksheet so students are in a mental computation mind-set. Always encourage them to invent strategies and to share their thinking with the class. Ask questions that will stimulate thinking about strategies presented in the worksheet but not yet mentioned by a student. This discussion serves as a rehearsal for what is to come. It will help to assure success and mastery of skills.

The intent of the following suggestions is to help you to be flexible given the uniqueness of each worksheet. Use the suggestions in any combination that makes the best sense to you.

* Be familiar with the task and strategy *before* assigning worksheets to students.

* Make overhead transparencies not only for the pages with the overhead symbol, but for other student pages as well if you feel this will help your students.

* At other times you may want to copy two to three examples from the student page on the chalkboard. Be sure that all the different strategies are represented. Use these examples as a basis for class discussion.

* You may want to work through the first example on a worksheet with your students.

* Introduce the **Four Basic Strategies** (see pages 7–10) into the discussion.

Bridge the Ten:
A BASIC STEP

○ ○ ○ ○ ○ ○ ○ ○ ○ ○ ○ ○

A *basic* step in mental computation is adding a **one**-digit number to a **two**-digit number with bridging (connecting) into the next decade.

EXAMPLES:

58
+ 4 $\rightarrow$

1.
8 + 4 = 12
Think: 2

2.
Think the next decade:
50 $\longrightarrow$ 60

3.
The answer is:
62.

47
+ 6 $\rightarrow$

1.
7 + 6 = 13
Think: 3

2.
Think the next decade:
40 $\longrightarrow$ 50

3.
The answer is:
53.

The most important idea to remember is that the next decade is bridged (connected) without the formal carrying step.

You can combine bridging the decade with multiplication:

EXAMPLE:

3 x 8 + 7
   24 + 7

1. 4 + 7 = 11
Think: 1

2. Think the next decade:
20 → 30

3. The answer is 31.

Mentally compute. Bridge to the next decade.

1. 63
    + 9

2. 34
    + 7

3. 109
    + 12

4. 84
    + 8

5. 4 x 9 + 5 = _____

6. 6 x 9 + 8 = _____

7. 8 x 8 + 7 = _____

8. 5 x 7 + 6 = _____

Name _____

Don't Carry That 10—Bridge It!

Mentally compute. Add the center number to each of the numbers outside the circle. Bridge to the next decade.

1.
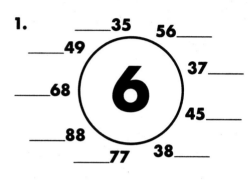
_____35 56_____
_____49
_____68 6 37_____
_____88 45_____
_____77 38_____

2.
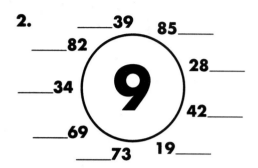
_____39 85_____
_____82
_____34 9 28_____
_____69 42_____
_____73 19_____

3.

_____19 76_____
_____87
_____36 5 18_____
_____49 29_____
_____66 77_____

4.
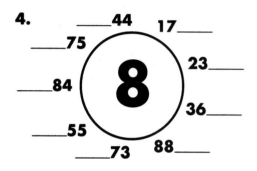
_____44 17_____
_____75
_____84 8 23_____
_____55 36_____
_____73 88_____

5.
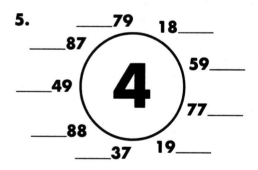
_____79 18_____
_____87
_____49 4 59_____
_____88 77_____
_____37 19_____

6.
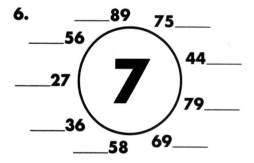
_____89 75_____
_____56
_____27 7 44_____
_____36 79_____
_____58 69_____

7.
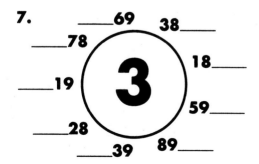
_____69 38_____
_____78
_____19 3 18_____
_____28 59_____
_____39 89_____

Addition Strategies Make for Quick and Easy Addition

You can add numbers very *quickly* and *easily*. You just need to be familiar with different strategies. Below are five addition strategies you can use. Remember that different examples may require different strategies.

STRATEGY 1   *Break up one number.*

36 + 25	78 + 29	155 + 34
36 + (20 + 5)	78 + (20 + 9)	155 + (30 + 4)
56 + 5	98 + 9	185 + 4
61	107	189

STRATEGY 2   *Break up two numbers.*

36 + 25	78 + 29	155 + 34
(30 + 6) + (20 + 5)	(70 + 8) + (20 + 9)	(150 + 5) + (30 + 4)
(30 + 20) + (6 + 5)	(70 + 20) + (8 + 9)	(150 + 30) + (5 + 4)
50 + 11	90 + 17	180 + 9
61	107	189

STRATEGY 3   *Count by 10's.*

36 + 25	78 + 29	155 + 34
36 + 10 + 10 + 5	78 + 10 + 10 + 9	155 + 10 + 10 + 10 + 4
36 → 46 → 56 + 5	78 → 88 → 98 + 9	155 →165 →175 →185 + 4
61	107	189

STRATEGY 4   *Make a 10's number.*

44 + 29	39 + 179	65 + 28	125 + 86
44 + (30 -1)	(40 -1) + (180 -1)	65 + (30 -2)	125+ (75 + 11)
(44 + 30) - 1	(40 + 180) + (-1 + -1)	(65 + 30) - 2	(125 + 75) + 11
74 - 1	220 + (-2)	95 - 2	200 + 11
73	218	93	211

STRATEGY 5   *Adjust both numbers.*

29 + 44	27 + 146	125 + 86	125 + 86
(30 + 1) + (44 - 1)	(27 + 3) + (146 - 3)	(125 + 5) + (86 - 5)	(125 - 4) + (86 + 4)
30 + 43	30 + 143	130 + 81	121 + 90
73	30 + (140 + 3)	130 + (80 + 1) **OR**	(120 + 1) + 90
	(30 + 140) + 3	(130 + 80) + 1	(120 + 90) + 1
	170 + 3	210 + 1	210 + 1
	173	211	211

Name _____

Using Addition Strategies

Add the following mentally. Use an addition strategy that makes adding quick and easy. Resist trying to use your regular method for adding. With practice you will see how fast you really can add. Remember that often more than one strategy can be used. Choose those that work best for you.

1. 21 + 43 = _____   **2.** 43 + 11 = _____   **3.** 34 + 23 = _____

4. 14 + 37 = _____   **5.** 19 + 38 = _____   **6.** 32 + 30 = _____

7. 32 + 12 = _____   **8.** 64 + 28 = _____   **9.** 29 + 68 = _____

10. 58 + 29 = _____   **11.** 12 + 49 = _____   **12.** 24 + 29 = _____

13. 75 + 42 = _____   **14.** 62 + 20 = _____   **15.** 50 + 47 = _____

16. 25
      + 38

17. 44
      + 17

18. 88
      + 39

19. 76
      + 18

20. 48
      + 48

21. 85
      + 25

22. 76
      + 87

23. 146
      + 37

24. 223
      + 29

25. 137
      + 48

26. 74
      + 65

27. 68
      + 27

28. 127 + 14 = _____   **29.** 263 + 28 = _____   **30.** 588 + 40 = _____

Name _____

Adding Nice Numbers

o o o o o o o o o o o o o o o o o o o o o o o o o o o o o o o

> **Teacher:** How did you add 326 + 99 so quickly?
>
> **Mark:** I added <u>100</u> to 326 and got 426. Then I subtracted 1 from the answer.
>
> **Kelly:** I added 100 to <u>325</u> and quickly got 425. I like to adjust my numbers ahead of time. You can either subtract the <u>1</u> now or later. I prefer doing it now.
>
> **Tracy:** I don't do anything. I just look at the numbers and know that the answer is 425.

Quickly add by thinking the answer. Think hundreds to make adding easier.

1. 673 + 99 = _____   **2.** 1,289 + 99 = _____

3. $3.48 + $1.95 = _____   **4.** 235 + 99 = _____

5. 2,678 + 99 = _____   **6.** 276 + 99 + 99 = _____

7. 99 + 456 = _____   **8.** 5,479 + 199 = _____

9. 127 + 98 + 99 = _____   **10.** 723 + 299 = _____

11. 721
      + 99

12. 8,647
      + 198

13. 299
        98
       + 97

14. 4,886
      + 1,998

ADDING NICER NUMBERS

Think the addition to do it quickly and easily. Develop your own strategy .

15. 426 + 101 = _____   **16.** 96 + 101 = _____   **17.** 235 + 101 = _____

18. 12 + 101 = _____   **19.** 760 + 101 = _____   **20.** 457 + 101 = _____

21. 923 + 101 = _____   **22.** 684 + 102 = _____   **23.** 128 + 103 = _____

24. 539 + 104 = _____   **25.** 816 + 105 = _____   **26.** 2,487 + 1,001 = _____

What strategies did you develop?

Name _____

Pick A Pair

13 * 20 * 22 * 25 * 30 * 31 * 69 * 70 * 75 * 80 * 82

Do all work *mentally*. Fill in the spaces with the above number(s) that give the following sums:

1. __22__ + _____ = **52**   2. _____ + _____ = **88**

3. _____ + __25__ = **45**   4. _____ + _____ = **110**

5. __20__ + _____ = **90**   6. _____ + _____ = **152**

7. _____ + _____ = **100**   8. _____ + _____ = **101**

9. __25__ + _____ = **105**   10. _____ + _____ = **107**

11. _____ + _____ = **38**   12. _____ + _____ = **112**

13. __69__ + _____ = **89**   14. _____ + _____ = **151**

15. _____ + __82__ = **157**   16. _____ + _____ = **150**

17. _____ + _____ = **113**   18. _____ + _____ = **92**

19. _____ + _____ = **104**   20. _____ + _____ = **149**

Name _____

Subtraction Strategies Make for Quick and Easy Subtraction

You also can subtract numbers very quickly and easily. Again, you just need to be familiar with different strategies. Below are **three** strategies you can use. Study and then practice them.

STRATEGY 1 *Decompose or breakdown numbers.*

47 - 15	83 - 27	91 - 67
47 - (10 - 5)	83 - (20 - 7)	91 - (60 - 7)
(47 - 10) - 5	(83 - 20) - 7	(91 - 60) - 7
37 - 5	63 - 7	31 - 7
32	56	24

1. 36 - 12 = _____   **2.** 84 - 41 = _____   **3.** 63 - 38 = _____

4. 58 - 24 = _____   **5.** 97 - 64 = _____   **6.** 71 - 52 = _____

STRATEGY 2 *Make a 10's number by adjusting both numbers.*

56 - 19	74 - 31	81 - 27
(56 + 1) - (19 + 1)	(74 - 1) - (31 - 1)	(81 + 3) - (27 + 3)
57 - 20	73 - 30	84 - 30
37	43	54

1. 94 - 19 = _____   **2.** 64 - 39 = _____   **3.** 245 - 79 = _____

4. 47 - 29 = _____   **5.** 51 - 28 = _____   **6.** 188 - 42 = _____

STRATEGY 3 *Count up! (It's like you're counting change.)*

54 - 36	185 - 93	400 - 187
from 36 count to 54	from 93 count to 185	from 187 count to 400
36 → 40 (4)	93 → 100 (7)	187 → 200 (13)
40 → 50 (10)	100 → 185 (85)	200 → 400 (200)
50 → 54 (4)	7 + 85	213
4 + 10 + 4	92	
18		

1. 50 - 28 = _____   **2.** 125 - 96 = _____   **3.** 716 - 650 = _____

4. 47 - 31 = _____   **5.** 345 - 198 = _____   **6.** 845 - 685 = _____

Name _____

Subtracting Nice Numbers

ooooooooooooooooooooooooooooooooooooooo

> **Teacher:** How did you subtract 99 from 614 so quickly?
>
> **Mark:** I subtracted <u>100</u> from 614. Then I added 1 to the answer 514 to get 515.
>
> **Linda:** I subtracted <u>100</u> from <u>615</u>. I added 1 to each number before I subtracted.
>
> **Kelly:** I just knew the answer was 515.
>
> **Alex:** When I subtract a 9 from the number in the ones place, I know I'm going to get a number that's one more than the number I subtracted from. Since I know that, I just subtract 100 and add 1 to the number in the ones place.

Subtract mentally. Use one of the above strategies.

1. 763 - 99 = _____   **2.** 219 - 99 = _____   **3.** 578 - 99 = _____

4. 334 - 99 = _____   **5.** 755 - 99 = _____   **6.** 947 - 99 = _____

7. 853 - 99 = _____   **8.** 285 - 98 = _____   **9.** 518 - 98 = _____

10. 591 - 97 = _____   **11.** 674 - 95 = _____   **12.** 602 - 97 = _____

13. 625   **14.** 256   **15.** 169   **16.** 782   **17.** 393
        - 99   - 99   - 99   - 199   - 199

18. 462   **19.** 588   **20.** 755   **21.** 4,671   **22.** 7,631
        -299   - 197   - 198   - 195   - 199

~~~~~~

SUBTRACTING NICER NUMBERS

Think the subtraction to do it quickly and easily. Develop your own strategy.

1. 426 - 101 = _____   **2.** 394 - 101 = _____   **3.** 235 - 101 = _____

4. 612 - 101 = _____   **5.** 760 - 101 = _____   **6.** 457 - 101 = _____

7. 923 - 101 = _____   **8.** 684 - 102 = _____   **9.** 128 - 103 = _____

10. 538 - 104 = _____   **11.** 816 - 105 = _____   **12.** 2,487 - 1,001 = _____

What strategies did you develop?

Name _____

Instant Subtraction:
SUBTRACTING FROM A NUMBER THAT IS A POWER OF TEN

This is what you will be able to do *instantly* when you understand the principles of complements.

100	1,000	10,000	100,000	1,000,000
- 32	- 472	- 6,253	- 57,134	- 256,247

✱ First, you need to be able to recall the complements that make 9 and 10.

✱ When subtracting from 100, the answer in the tens place will be the complement of the number in the tens place being subtracted to equal 9. The answer in the ones place will be the complement of the ones place number being subtracted to equal 10.

✱ In the example at right, in the tens place, the 5 is the complement of 4 to equal 9. In the ones place, the 8 is the complement of 2 to make 10.

EXAMPLE:
$100 - 42 = 58$

```
  1 0 0
-   4 2
  5 8
  ↓ ↓
  9 10
```

✱ Let's see if you have it yet. When you try 100 - 74 = _2_ _6_, the answer digit in the tens place is 2 because it is the complement of 7 to yield 9. The answer digit in the ones place is 6 because it is the complement of 4 to yield 10.

Let's practice! Write down the answer in the tens place first. Then write the ones digit.

1. 100 - 38 = __ __   **2.** 100 - 86 = __ __   **3.** 100 - 62 = __ __

4. 100 - 34 = __ __   **5.** 100 - 55 = __ __   **6.** 100 - 43 = __ __

You can use the complementary strategies with all the numbers that are powers of 10. Try these for practice:

7. 1,000 - 462 = _____   **8.** 1,000 - 847 = _____

9. 1,000 - 601 = _____   **10.** 1,000 - 338 = _____

11. 10,000 - 5,132 = _____   **12.** 10,000 - 8,351 = _____

13. 10,000	**14.** 100,000	**15.** 100,000	**16.** 1,000,000
-2,348	- 88,386	- 25,764	- 467,892

17. 1,000,000	**18.** 1,000,000	**19.** 1,000,000	**20.** 10,000
- 845,625	- 732,561	- 204,567	-3,400

Now try the examples at the top of the page!

Name _____

Pick a Pair

o o o o o o o o o o o o o o o o

13 * 20 * 22 * 24 * 25 * 30 * 31 * 69 * 70 * 75 * 80 * 82

Do all work mentally. Fill in the spaces with the above number(s) that give the following sums:

1. _____ - _____ = **10**   **2.** _____ - _____ = **45**

3. _____ - _____ = **50**   **4.** _82_ - _____ = **57**

5. _____ - _13_ = **17**   **6.** _____ - _69_ = **6**

7. _____ - _____ = **3**   **8.** _____ - _____ = **40**

9. _____ - _22_ = **53**   **10.** _____ - _____ = **8**

11. _82_ - _____ = **69**   **12.** _____ - _____ = **11**

13. _____ - _____ = **7**   **14.** _____ - _22_ = **58**

15. _____ - _____ = **44**   **16.** _____ - _22_ = **47**

17. _____ - _13_ = **18**   **18.** _____ - _____ = **55**

19. _____ - _____ = **60**   **20.** _80_ - _____ = **49**

37

Name _____

Eleven is Magic!

o o o o o o o o o o o o o o o o o o o o o o o o o

Multiplication by 11 is MAGICAL! Here's how!

The Mental Magic Way:		**The Long Way:**

② 5 ③
(x   1 1)
  2 7 8 3

→ 3 + 5
→ 5 + 2

Start from the right.
1. Write down the 3.
2. Add the 3 + 5.
3. Add the 5 + 2.
4. Write down the 2.

  2 5 3
x   1 1
  2 5 3
  2 5 3
  2 7 8 3

The Mental Magic Way:

① 4 3 6 ②
(x   1 1)
  1 5 7 9 8 2

→ 2 + 6
→ 6 + 3
→ 3 + 4
→ 4 + 1

The Long Way:

    1 4 3 6 2
x   1 1
    1 4 3 6 2
  1 4 3 6 2
  1 5 7 9 8 2

The Mental Magic Way:

⑥ 7 ⑤
(x   1 1)
  7 4 2 5

→ 5 +7 + = 12
(Carry the 1 to the next pair.)
→ 7 + 6 + (the carried 1) = 14
(Carry the 1 to the next number.)
→ Add the carried 1 to the 6.

The Long Way:

    6 7 5
x   1 1
    6 7 5
  6 7 5
  7 4 2 5

Try your hand at magic!

1. 11 x 32 = _____

2. 11 x 68 = _____

3. 11 x 3,071 = _____

4. 11 x 425 = _____

5. 11 x 359 = _____

6. 4,188 x 11 = _____

7. 11 x 3,626 = _____

8. 11 x 2,875 = _____

9. 11 x 9,876 = _____

10. 11 x 723,524 = _____

11. 11 x 23,658 = _____

12. 34,807 x 11 = _____

Powerful Multiplication:
MULTIPLICATION BY POWERS OF TEN

○ ○

Think you'll ever be able to compute 243 x 1,000 mentally? What about 10,000 x 1,000? You can! Here's how!

Let's *cut* and *paste*!

$8 \times 10 = 80$ *Cut* the zero from the 10 and *paste* it after the 8.
$8 \times 100 = 800$ *Cut* the two zeroes from the 100 and *paste* them after the 8.
$8 \times 1,000 = 8,000$ *Cut* the three zeroes from the 1,000 and *paste* them after the 8.

The rule is: When multiplying by powers of 10, count the number of zeroes. Attach that number of zeroes to the number you are multiplying.

Try these:

$7 \times 10 =$ _____ $400 \times 10 =$ _____ $1,000 \times 100 =$ _____

For the rest of this powerful multiplication, we turn to a classroom conversation.

Marianne: I can multiply 30 x 50 in my head!

Teacher: Tell us how you do it!

Marianne: Well, 30 is 3 x 10 and 50 is 5 x 10. So, I actually have 3 x 5 x 10 x 10 or 15 x 100 or 1,500.

Todd: It gets even easier! To multiply 30 x 50 just multiply the 3 x 5 and attach the two zeroes. You get 15 and two zeroes attached to make 1,500.

Marianne: I like that. So with 60 x 80, I would think 6 x 8 is 48 and then attach the two zeroes.

---

1. $70 \times 90 =$ _____   **2.** $40 \times 50 =$ _____   **3.** $60 \times 30 =$ _____

4. $80 \times 70 =$ _____   **5.** $25 \times 30 =$ _____   **6.** $60 \times 300 =$ _____

7. $900 \times 40 =$ _____   **8.** $700 \times 50 =$ _____   **9.** $2,400 \times 20 =$ _____

10. $18 \times 200 =$ _____   **11.** $400 \times 300 =$ _____   **12.** $900 \times 5,000 =$ _____

13. $4,000 \times 25 =$ _____   **14.** $20 \times 30 \times 50 =$ _____

15. $90 \times 10 \times 40 =$ _____   **16.** $400 \times 30 \times 20 =$ _____

17. $80 \times 20 \times 20 =$ _____   **18.** $5 \times 3 \times 20 \times 10 =$ _____

19. $25 \times 100 \times 4 =$ _____   **20.** $50 \times 2 \times 700 =$ _____

Quick and Easy
Multiplication by 5, 50, and 500

You will find that multiplying mentally by 5, 50, and 500 is *quick*, *easy,* and *fun*!

Here's how:

To multiply	5×842	(Multiply 842 by 10 and then divide by 2.)
	8,420	(Mentally attach a zero.)
	$8,420 \div 2$	(Then divide by 2.)
	4,210	
To multiply	50×648	(Multiply 648 by 100 and then divide by 2.)
	64,800	(Mentally attach 2 zeroes.)
	$64,800 \div 2$	(Then divide by 2.)
	32,400	
To multiply	500×268	(Multiply 268 by 1,000 and then divide by 2.)
	268,000	(Mentally attach 3 zeroes.)
	$268,000 \div 2$	(Then divide by 2.)
	134,000	

Using the strategies you've learned, try these:

1. $5 \times 444 =$ _____

2. $50 \times 86 =$ _____

3. $500 \times 64 =$ _____

4. $624 \times 5 =$ _____

5. $50 \times 24 =$ _____

6. $42 \times 500 =$ _____

7. $864 \times 5 =$ _____

8. $36 \times 50 =$ _____

9. $812 \times 500 =$ _____

10. $5 \times 152 =$ _____

11. $50 \times 48 =$ _____

12. $500 \times 72 =$ _____

13. $5 \times 135 =$ _____

14. $50 \times 27 =$ _____

15. $500 \times 19 =$ _____

16. $81 \times 50 =$ _____

Name _____

Multiply Mentally by 9, 99, 999

Some students think that it is easier to multiply mentally by 99 and 999 than it is to multiply mentally by 9. What do you think?

Let's multiply by 99.

EXAMPLE 1
46 x 99 = 46 x (100 - 1)
        (Rename 99 as 100 - 1.)
    = 4,600 - 46 (Think 600 - 46.)
    = 4,554
The thinking process is shortened to 4,600 - 46 = 4,554.

EXAMPLE 2
72 x 99
This shortens to 7,200 - 72 = 7,128

Now, we'll multiply by 999.

EXAMPLE 1
24 x 999 = 24 x (1000 - 1)
       (Rename 999 as 1,000 - 1
    = 24,000 - 24 (Think 4,000 - 24.)
    = 23,976
The thinking process is shortened to 24,000 - 24 = 23,976.

EXAMPLE 2
83 x 999
This shortens to 83,000 - 83 = 82,917.

Use this thinking pattern for multiplying mentally by 9.

EXAMPLE 1
36 x 9 = 36 x (10 - 1) (Rename 9 as 10 - 1.)
    = 360 - 36 (Think 60 - 36.)
    = 324
This shortens to 360 - 36 = 324.

EXAMPLE 2
41 x 9
This shortens to 410 - 41 = 369.

My students said that the subtraction step was too much of a mental load. They came up with the following idea.

EXAMPLE 1
36 x 9
First, multiply the tens by 9 (9 x 3 tens = 270).
Next, multiply the ones by 9 (9 x 6 ones = 54).
Then, add the two products mentally
(270 + 54 = 324).

EXAMPLE 2
36 x 9
This shortens to:
3 tens x 9 = 270,
9 x 6 = 54, 270 + 54 = 324

Do the following multiplication mentally.

1. 99 x 5 = _____   **2.** 999 x 4 = _____   **3.** 9 x 24 = _____

4. 999 x 36 = _____   **5.** 16 x 99 = _____   **6.** 12 x 999 = _____

41

Name _____

Other Multiplication Short Cuts

You can also shorten other multiplication problems. Here's how you can multiply mentally 7 x 395:

> 7 x 395 = 7 x (400 - 5)
> = 2,800 - 35
> = 2,765
> This shortens to 2,800 - 35.

Try these:

1. 6 x $1.95 = _____   **2.** 12 x 95 = _____   **3.** 299 x 8 = _____

4. 3 x 295 = _____   **5.** $9.95 x 9 = _____   **6.** 99 x 12 = _____

7. 4 x $5.95 = _____   **8.** 25 x $1.99 = _____   **9.** 6 x 599 = _____

Here's a new strategy for you. You can double *one factor and* halve *the other factor to get numbers that are easily manageable.*

> **EXAMPLES:**   4 x 50 = 200   4 x 65 = 260
> ($\frac{1}{2}$ of 4) 2 x 100 (double 50) = 200   ($\frac{1}{2}$ of 4) 2 x 130 (double 65) = 260

Halve and double until you get a pair of numbers that are manageable for you to compute mentally.

1. 24 x 25 = _____   **2.** 50 x 64 = _____   **3.** 8 x 350 = _____

4. 45 x 12 = _____   **5.** 32 x 8 = _____   **6.** 25 x 36 = _____

7. 8 x 35 = _____   **8.** 25 x 92 = _____   **9.** 8 x 125 = _____

10. 65 x 4 = _____   **11.** 8 x 45 = _____   **12.** 18 x 25 = _____

13. 25 x 8 = _____   **14.** 24 x 250 = _____   **15.** 6 x 35 = _____

16. 6 x 12 = _____   **17.** 48 x 25 = _____   **18.** 72 x 25 = _____

Name _____

Follow Me

○ ○ ○ ○ ○ ○ ○ ○ ○ ○ ○ ○ ○ ○

**10 * 11 * 13 * 20 * 22 * 25 * 30
31 * 69 * 70 * 75 * 80 * 82**

Do all work *mentally*. Fill in the spaces with the above factor(s) that give the following products:

1. _____ x _____ = 690   2. _____ x _____ = 660

3. _____ x _____ = 600   4. _____ x _____ = 2,100

5. _____ x _____ = 5,600   6. _____ x _____ = 220

7. _____ x _____ = 1,600   8. _____ x _____ = 902

9. _____ x _____ = 242   10. _____ x _____ = 500

11. _____ x _____ = 260   12. _____ x _____ = 820

13. _____ x _____ = 620   14. _____ x _____ = 390

15. _____ x _____ = 275   16. _____ x _____ = 759

17. _____ x _____ = 750   18. _____ x _____ = 880

19. _____ x _____ = 1,400   20. _____ x _____ = 300

Name _____

Give Me What's Left

Follow the steps as the teacher reads them. Do this practice work orally.

STEP 1: Which example in box I has no remainder?
Which example in box II has no remainder?

STEP 2: Which example in box I has the largest remainder?
Which example in box II has the largest remainder?

STEP 3: Look at each example.
Give me what's left after you divide.

I

$5 \div 2$	$4\overline{)6}$	$10 \div 3$	$8 \div 5$	$5\overline{)14}$	$18 \div 7$
$6\overline{)15}$	$12 \div 5$	$7\overline{)13}$	$9\overline{)16}$	$10 \div 5$	$9 \div 4$

II

$20 \div 6$	$5\overline{)21}$	$24 \div 7$	$6\overline{)28}$	$8\overline{)33}$	$27 \div 5$
$32 \div 7$	$35 \div 8$	$9\overline{)36}$	$40 \div 6$	$7\ 48$	$32 \div 6$

III

$40 \div 7$	$63 \div 8$	$47 \div 7$	$57 \div 7$	$55 \div 9$	$70 \div 8$
$48 \div 6$	$71 \div 8$	$70 \div 9$	$80 \div 9$	$64 \div 8$	$85 \div 9$

In the space provided, write what's left after you divide.

1. $6 \div 5$ _____

2. $20 \div 4$ _____

3. $6\overline{)42}$ _____

4. $44 \div 5$ _____

5. $2\overline{)7}$ _____

6. $21 \div 5$ _____

7. $9\overline{)40}$ _____

8. $28 \div 7$ _____

9. $4 \div 4$ _____

10. $9\overline{)24}$ _____

11. $54 \div 9$ _____

12. $9\overline{)60}$ _____

13. $6\overline{)9}$ _____

14. $18 \div 6$ _____

15. $41 \div 8$ _____

16. $5\overline{)48}$ _____

17. $6 \div 4$ _____

18. $5\overline{)34}$ _____

19. $7\overline{)43}$ _____

20. $75 \div 9$ _____

21. $10 \div 6$ _____

Name _____

Look and Say: Short Division

This exercise is to improve your skill with doing short division *mentally*. LOOK at the example and then SAY the answer.

1. 2)248   **2.** 6)180   **3.** 250 ÷ 5   **4.** 9)999   **5.** 2)482

6. 5)405   **7.** 9)369   **8.** 246 ÷ 6   **9.** 497 ÷ 7   **10.** 480 ÷8

11. 8)728   **12.** 2)842   **13.** 357 ÷7   **14.** 6)300   **15.** 8)560

16. 720 ÷ 9 **17.** 963 ÷ 3 **18.** 3)300   **19.** 108 ÷ 2   **20.** 5)355

21. 368 ÷ 4 **22.** 2)642   **23.** 8)888   **24.** 8)648   **25.** 4)484

26. 639 ÷ 3 **27.** 486 ÷ 6 **28.** 4)816   **29.** 3)369   **30.** 129 ÷ 3

Match the examples on the left with the answers on the right. Place the letter of the correct answer in the answer space.

____ **1.** 2)2,764   **A.** 821   ____**11.** 4)4,328   **A.** 473

____ **2.** 4)1,444   **B.** 346   ____**12.** 3)9,276   **B.** 309

____ **3.** 8)1,832   **C.** 3,581   ____**13.** 8)2,472   **C.** 451

____ **4.** 5)4,105   **D.** 305   ____**14.** 7)3,479   **D.** 841

____ **5.** 7)2,135   **E.** 1,061   ____**15.** 9)4,059   **E.** 383

____ **6.** 9)2,529   **F.** 1,382   ____**16.** 6)4,146   **F.** 3,092

____ **7.** 6)6,366   **G.** 229   ____**17.** 8)4,008   **G.** 501

____ **8.** 5)1,650   **H.** 361   ____**18.** 3)1,419   **H.** 691

____ **9.** 7)2,422   **I.** 330   ____**19.** 9)3,447   **I.** 1,082

____**10.** 2)7,162   **J.** 281   ____**20.** 6)5,046   **J.** 497

45

Name _____

Jeopardy Division

○ ○

JEOPARDY ANSWER: 350 ÷ 70 (from the JEOPARDY ANSWER BOARD below)

JEOPARDY QUESTION: What is 5? (The Jeopardy Answer 350 ÷ 70 is written under "What is 5?" in the **JEOPARDY QUESTIONS** below.)

Are you ready? Then begin the game! As the answer is real out loud, write it below the correct Jeopardy question.

JEOPARDY ANSWER BOARD

350 ÷ 70	40)120	450 ÷ 50	36 ÷ 4	40)80	320 ÷ 80
490 ÷ 70	3)12	90)540	90)720	120 ÷ 30	280 ÷ 40
63 ÷ 7	240 ÷ 40	4)8	210 ÷ 70	60)480	240 ÷ 30
35 ÷ 7	7)42	350 ÷ 50	8)40	60)120	90)270

JEOPARDY QUESTIONS

What is **2**?	What is **3**?	What is **4**?	What is **5**?
1. _____	1. _____	1. _____	1. _350 ÷ 70_
2. _____	2. _____	2. _____	2. _____
3. _____	3. _____	3. _____	3. _____

What is **6**?	What is **7**?	What is **8**?	What is **9**?
1. _____	1. _____	1. _____	1. _____
2. _____	2. _____	2. _____	2. _____
3. _____	3. _____	3. _____	3. _____

Name _____

Pick A Pair

3 * 4 * 5 * 6 * 7 * 8 * 9 * 40 * 60 * 70 * 80

Do all work *mentally*. Fill in with a number(s) from above to make a correct math sentence.

1. ___90___ ÷ ___10___ = _____

2. _____ ÷ _____ = **14**

3. ___100___ ÷ ___20___ = _____

4. ___4,200___ ÷ _____ = _____

5. _____ ÷ ___5___ = **8**

6. _____ ÷ _____ = **2**

7. ___70___ ÷ _____ = **14**

8. ___90___ ÷ ___30___ = _____

9. _____ ÷ ___10___ = **6**

10. ___490___ ÷ _____ = **70**

11. ___90___ ÷ ___18___ = _____

12. _____ ÷ _____ = **5**

13. ___180___ ÷ _____ = **3**

14. ___72___ ÷ _____ = **9**

15. ___640___ ÷ _____ = **8**

16. _____ ÷ _____ = **10**

17. ___360___ ÷ _____ = **9**

18. ___4,800___ ÷ _____ = **80**

19. ___360___ ÷ _____ = **6**

20. ___390___ ÷ ___130___ = _____

You are strongly encouraged to read the teaching suggestions in **USING MENTAL COMPUTATION WITH WHOLE NUMBERS** on page 27. The suggestions there also apply to fractions.

Below are additional hints which need to be emphasized throughout *mental* work with fractions.

* Encourage pupils to share their thinking with the class.

* Fractions can have many names.

$$\frac{1}{2} = \frac{2}{4} \qquad\qquad \frac{3}{6} = \frac{4}{8} \qquad\qquad \frac{2}{4} = \frac{3}{6} = \frac{4}{8}$$

$$1 = \frac{3}{3} \qquad\qquad 1 = \frac{8}{8} \qquad\qquad \frac{3}{3} = \frac{8}{8} = \frac{12}{12}$$

$$2\frac{1}{2} = \frac{5}{2} \qquad\qquad \frac{7}{3} = 2\frac{1}{3}$$

* Mentally rename fractions to higher and lower terms.

$$\frac{3}{4} = \frac{6}{8} \qquad\qquad \frac{1}{2} = \frac{5}{10} \qquad\qquad \frac{2}{4} = \frac{6}{12}$$

$$\frac{14}{16} = \frac{7}{8} \qquad\qquad 2\frac{6}{10} = 2\frac{3}{5}$$

* Mentally rename wholes.

$$\frac{2}{3} + \frac{2}{3} = 1\frac{1}{3} \qquad 2\frac{5}{4} = 3\frac{1}{4} \qquad \frac{6}{8} + \frac{1}{4} + \frac{1}{2} = 1\frac{1}{2}$$

$$3 = 2\frac{4}{4} = 2\frac{12}{12} \qquad 2\frac{1}{3} = 1\frac{4}{3} \qquad 5\frac{6}{10} = 4\frac{16}{10}$$

* Mentally multiplying a whole number by a unit fraction is the same as dividing the whole number by the denominator in the unit fraction.

$$\frac{1}{3} \times 18 = 18 \div 3 = 6 \qquad\qquad \frac{1}{5} \times 15 = 15 \div 5 = 3$$

* Mentally dividing fractions is similar to the meaning of the standard division algorithm for whole numbers.
How many of a particular size (divisor) are contained in the dividend?

$$2\frac{3}{4} \div \frac{1}{8} = \frac{1}{8}\overline{)2\frac{3}{4}} = \frac{1}{8}\overline{)2\frac{6}{8}} = 22$$

Name _____

Adding Fractions: Key Ideas

○ ○

Here are four **key ideas** to help you **ADD FRACTIONS MENTALLY:**

You need to be a flexible thinker so you can see that a fraction may have many different names.

Fractions that **equal** $\frac{1}{2}$ have **numerators** that are $\frac{1}{2}$ their **denominators**, or denominators that are twice their numerators.

$$\frac{1}{2} = \frac{2}{4}, \quad \frac{1}{2} = \frac{3}{6}, \quad \frac{1}{2} = \frac{2}{4}, \quad \frac{1}{2} = \frac{5}{10}$$

Unit fractions that are changed to higher terms ($\frac{1}{2}$ **piece** sizes such as thirds to sixths, fourths to eighths) always have numerators of 2.

$$\frac{1}{3} = \frac{2}{6}, \quad \frac{1}{4} = \frac{2}{8}, \quad \frac{1}{5} = \frac{2}{10}$$

There are fraction equivalents that will be **useful** to **know**.

$$\frac{3}{4} = \frac{6}{8}, \quad \frac{2}{3} = \frac{4}{6}$$

USING KEY FRACTION IDEAS

Use the KEY IDEAS to help you fill in the space below with the correct numerator or denominator.

1. $\frac{1}{2} = \frac{}{4}$ $\qquad$ $\frac{1}{2} = \frac{}{6}$ $\qquad$ $\frac{}{8} = \frac{1}{2}$ $\qquad$ $\frac{}{16} = \frac{1}{2}$

2. $\frac{1}{3} = \frac{}{6}$ $\qquad$ $\frac{2}{3} = \frac{}{6}$ $\qquad$ $\frac{1}{4} = \frac{}{8}$ $\qquad$ $\frac{2}{4} = \frac{}{8}$

3. $\frac{1}{5} = \frac{}{10}$ $\qquad$ $\frac{4}{10} = \frac{}{5}$ $\qquad$ $\frac{3}{5} = \frac{}{10}$ $\qquad$ $\frac{8}{} = \frac{4}{5}$

4. $\frac{1}{6} = \frac{}{12}$ $\qquad$ $\frac{4}{12} = \frac{}{6}$ $\qquad$ $\frac{}{12} = \frac{3}{6}$ $\qquad$ $\frac{8}{} = \frac{4}{6}$

5. $\frac{1}{2} + \frac{}{2} = 1$ $\qquad$ $\frac{1}{2} + \frac{}{4} = 1$ $\qquad$ $\frac{}{} + \frac{3}{6} = 1$ $\qquad$ $\frac{3}{} + \frac{2}{4} = 1$

6. $\frac{6}{} + \frac{5}{10} = 1$ $\qquad$ $\frac{4}{8} + \frac{}{12} = 1$ $\qquad$ $\frac{1}{3} + \frac{}{6} = \frac{2}{3}$ $\qquad$ $\frac{}{6} + \frac{1}{3} = 1$

7. $\frac{1}{4} + \frac{}{8} = \frac{3}{4}$ $\qquad$ $\frac{1}{5} + \frac{}{10} = \frac{2}{5}$ $\qquad$ $\frac{4}{10} + \frac{}{5} = \frac{3}{5}$ $\qquad$ $\frac{2}{5} + \frac{6}{} = 1$

Name _____

Finding the Compatible Partners

In the space provided in the circle, write the sum of the fractions. To help you to do these mentally, search for the COMPATIBLE PARTNERS that easily go together to make one whole.

EXAMPLE:

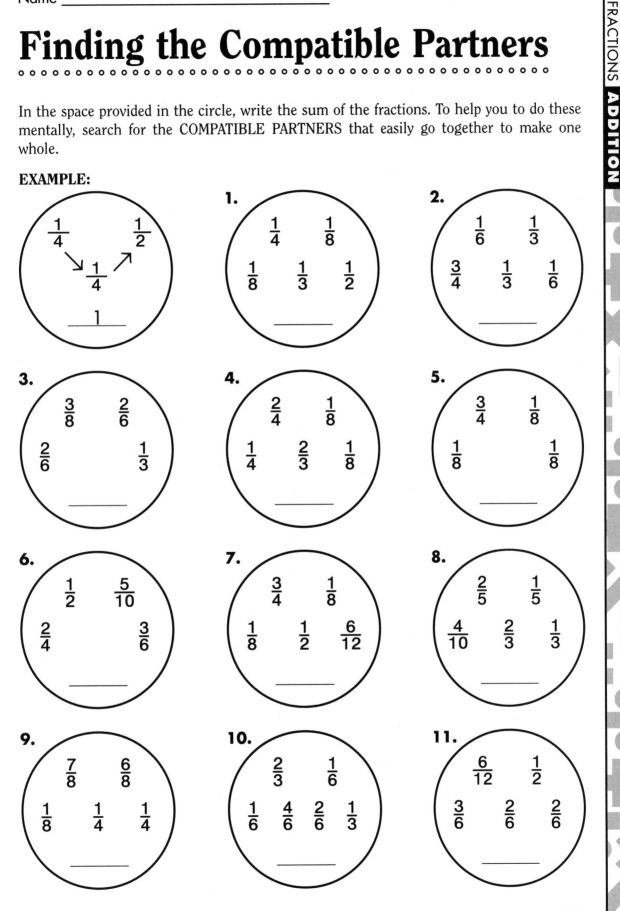

51

Name _____

Make One!

o o o o o o o o o o o o o o o

Choose a pair of like fractions that MAKE ONE when added together. Place the like fractions in the spaces below.

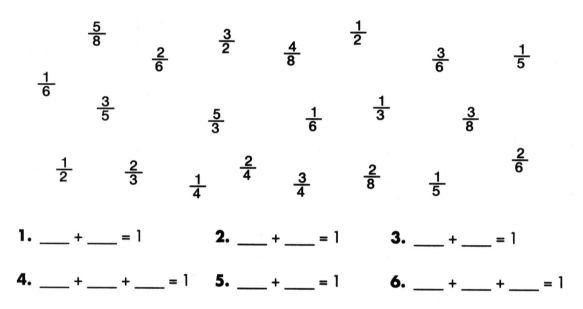

1. ___ + ___ = 1   **2.** ___ + ___ = 1   **3.** ___ + ___ = 1

4. ___ + ___ + ___ = 1   **5.** ___ + ___ = 1   **6.** ___ + ___ + ___ = 1

Choose a pair of unlike fractions that MAKE ONE when added together. You can use a fraction more than once.

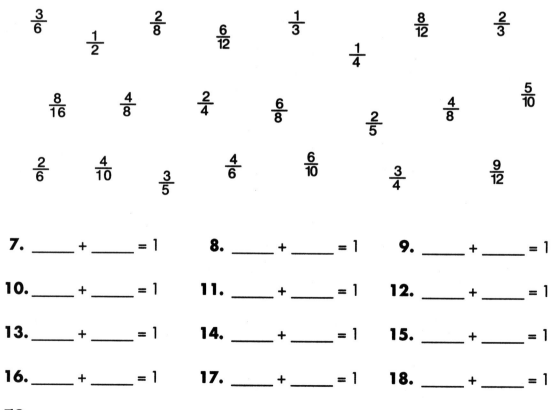

7. _____ + _____ = 1   **8.** _____ + _____ = 1   **9.** _____ + _____ = 1

10. _____ + _____ = 1   **11.** _____ + _____ = 1   **12.** _____ + _____ = 1

13. _____ + _____ = 1   **14.** _____ + _____ = 1   **15.** _____ + _____ = 1

16. _____ + _____ = 1   **17.** _____ + _____ = 1   **18.** _____ + _____ = 1

52

Name _____

Addition Strategies

Below are some strategies to help you mentally add both like and unlike fractions.

Mentally rename the $\frac{1}{2}$ as a fraction with the same denominator as the fraction you are adding.

EXAMPLE: $\frac{3}{4} + \frac{1}{2} = \frac{3}{4} + \frac{2}{4} = \frac{5}{4} = 1\frac{1}{4}$.

1. $\frac{1}{2} + \frac{1}{4} =$ _____

2. $\frac{1}{2} + \frac{2}{6} =$ _____

3. $\frac{3}{8} + \frac{1}{2} =$ _____

4. $\frac{4}{10} + \frac{1}{2} =$ _____

LOOK FOR THE $\frac{1}{2}$. It may have a different name such as $\frac{2}{4}, \frac{3}{6}, \frac{4}{8}$. Write your answers as mixed numbers.

5. $\frac{2}{6} + \frac{1}{2} =$ _____

6. $\frac{1}{2} + \frac{4}{6} =$ _____

7. $\frac{7}{12} + \frac{1}{2} =$ _____

8. $\frac{7}{8} + \frac{1}{2} =$ _____

9. $\frac{2}{6} + \frac{2}{4} =$ _____

10. $\frac{2}{4} + \frac{4}{6} =$ _____

11. $\frac{7}{12} + \frac{4}{8} =$ _____

12. $\frac{2}{4} + \frac{7}{8} =$ _____

Mentally add. Change the improper fractions in the answer to a mixed number.

13. $\frac{2}{3} + \frac{2}{3} =$ _____

14. $\frac{5}{6} + \frac{5}{6} =$ _____

15. $1\frac{4}{5} + 2\frac{3}{5} =$ _____

16. $3\frac{7}{10} + 2\frac{8}{10} =$ _____

17. $4\frac{7}{8} + 1\frac{4}{8} =$ _____

18. $\frac{2}{4} + \frac{2}{4} + \frac{1}{4} =$ _____

19. $\frac{5}{8} + \frac{6}{8} + \frac{4}{8} =$ _____

20. $\frac{7}{12} + \frac{6}{12} + \frac{2}{12} =$ _____

21. $1\frac{4}{5} + 1\frac{2}{5} + 2\frac{3}{5} =$ _____

22. $3\frac{4}{10} + 5\frac{9}{10} + 1\frac{4}{10} =$ _____

23. $\frac{7}{12} + \frac{6}{12} + \frac{11}{12} =$ _____

24. $2\frac{5}{6} + 2\frac{5}{6} + 2\frac{5}{6} =$ _____

Name _____

Using Addition Strategies

Mentally add the fractions. Be sure to **inspect** before you decide on the *strategy* or *strategies* involved. Remember:

     ✱ Make a whole. ($\frac{1}{8} + \frac{3}{4} + \frac{1}{8}$)

     ✱ Change unit fractions. ($\frac{1}{4} = \frac{2}{8}$)

     ✱ Change $\frac{1}{2}$ to a like denominator. ($\frac{3}{8} + \frac{1}{2} = \frac{3}{8} + \frac{4}{8} = \frac{7}{8}$)

     ✱ Look for $\frac{1}{2}$ in a different form ($\frac{1}{2} = \frac{2}{4}, \frac{3}{6}$, and so on.)

     ✱ Change the improper fraction to a mixed number. ($\frac{11}{8} = 1\frac{3}{8}$)

1. $\frac{7}{12}$
     $\frac{3}{12}$
$+ \frac{4}{12}$

2. $1\frac{4}{6}$
     $5\frac{3}{6}$
$+ 2\frac{2}{6}$

3. $1\frac{5}{8}$
     $4\frac{1}{8}$
     $2\frac{2}{8}$
$+ \frac{3}{8}$

4. $2\frac{3}{5}$
     $2\frac{4}{5}$
$+ 3\frac{4}{5}$

5. $3\frac{1}{2}$
$+ 1\frac{3}{4}$

6. $2\frac{5}{6}$
$+ 2\frac{4}{8}$

7. $2\frac{1}{2}$
     $1\frac{3}{6}$
$+ 2\frac{4}{5}$

8. $2\frac{3}{4}$
     $1\frac{2}{8}$
$+ 1\frac{3}{6}$

9. $3\frac{1}{4}$
     $2\frac{1}{8}$
$+ 5\frac{3}{4}$

10. $6\frac{4}{10}$
$+ 3\frac{9}{10}$

11. $4\frac{3}{4}$
     $2\frac{2}{8}$
$+ 1\frac{3}{4}$

12. $3\frac{2}{3}$
     $1\frac{2}{3}$
$+ \frac{4}{6}$

13. $3\frac{4}{6}$
     $1\frac{5}{8}$
$+ 2\frac{1}{3}$

14. $5\frac{2}{3}$
     $2\frac{7}{8}$
$+ 1\frac{2}{6}$

15. $4\frac{1}{6}$
     $2\frac{2}{12}$
$+ 3\frac{7}{12}$

16. $2\frac{6}{8}$
     $1\frac{3}{4}$
$+ \frac{2}{8}$

Name _____

Subtracting from Wholes

○ ○

To *mentally* subtract a fraction from one whole:
Think of a whole number as a fraction that can be renamed in many different ways. For example, 1 may equal $\frac{3}{3}, \frac{4}{4}, \frac{5}{5}, \frac{6}{6}$, and so on.

1. $1 - \frac{3}{4} =$ _____

2. $1 - \frac{2}{5} =$ _____

3. $1 - \frac{6}{10} =$ _____

4. $1 - \frac{1}{3} =$ _____

5. $1 - \frac{4}{6} =$ _____

6. $1 - \frac{5}{8} =$ _____

7. $\begin{array}{r} 1 \\ - \frac{3}{5} \\ \hline \end{array}$

8. $\begin{array}{r} 1 \\ - \frac{7}{12} \\ \hline \end{array}$

9. $\begin{array}{r} 1 \\ - \frac{9}{16} \\ \hline \end{array}$

To *mentally* subtract fractions from wholes:
Think of the wholes as mixed numbers. Rename the given whole number as one less, and then rename that one as a fraction. For example, $3 - \frac{1}{4}$ may be thought of as $2\frac{4}{4} - \frac{1}{4}$. Think of $5 - \frac{6}{8}$, as $4\frac{8}{8} - \frac{6}{8}$.

10. $2 - \frac{1}{4} =$ _____

11. $5 - \frac{3}{4} =$ _____

12. $3 - \frac{7}{8} =$ _____

13. $6 - \frac{4}{5} =$ _____

14. $2 - \frac{9}{16} =$ _____

15. $5 - \frac{8}{10} =$ _____

16. $\begin{array}{r} 4 \\ - \frac{2}{3} \\ \hline \end{array}$

17. $\begin{array}{r} 3 \\ - \frac{6}{8} \\ \hline \end{array}$

18. $\begin{array}{r} 5 \\ - \frac{4}{6} \\ \hline \end{array}$

Mentally subtract mixed numbers from wholes:
Follow the *strategy* used immediately above.
Think of $5 - 1\frac{2}{3}$ as $4\frac{3}{3} - 1\frac{2}{3}$. Think of $7 - 2\frac{1}{2}$, as $6\frac{2}{2} - 2\frac{1}{2}$.

19. $3 - 1\frac{1}{5} =$ _____

20. $4 - 1\frac{3}{8} =$ _____

21. $7 - 2\frac{4}{5} =$ _____

22. $8 - 3\frac{6}{10} =$ _____

23. $5 - 4\frac{6}{8} =$ _____

24. $3 - 1\frac{2}{3} =$ _____

25. $\begin{array}{r} 5 \\ - 3\frac{2}{8} \\ \hline \end{array}$

26. $\begin{array}{r} 6 \\ - 4\frac{2}{3} \\ \hline \end{array}$

27. $\begin{array}{r} 4 \\ - 2\frac{5}{6} \\ \hline \end{array}$

55

Name _____

In Your Head Subtraction

○ ○

Mentally rename the following fractions in preparation for the MENTAL SUBTRACTION to follow. Fill in the missing numerators.

1. $3 = 2\frac{}{4}$ **2.** $5 = 4\frac{}{8}$ **3.** $2 = 1\frac{}{3}$ **4.** $6 = 5\frac{}{12}$

5. $4 = 3\frac{}{16}$ **6.** $8 = 7\frac{}{5}$ **7.** $3 = 2\frac{}{6}$ **8.** $4 = 3\frac{}{10}$

9. $6\frac{1}{4} = 5\frac{}{4}$ **10.** $10\frac{2}{3} = 9\frac{}{3}$ **11.** $7\frac{3}{5} = 6\frac{}{5}$ **12.** $11\frac{6}{8} = 10\frac{}{8}$

13. $4\frac{3}{5} = 3\frac{}{5}$ **14.** $5\frac{4}{6} = 4\frac{}{6}$ **15.** $2\frac{3}{10} = 1\frac{}{10}$ **16.** $1\frac{12}{16} = \frac{}{16}$

Mentally SUBTRACT:
Rename the wholes and fractions *mentally*. **Think:** decrease the whole by 1 and increase the fraction portion by 1. To increase the fraction portion by 1, use $\frac{3}{3}, \frac{4}{4}, \frac{5}{5}$, and so on. For example, think of $6\frac{1}{3} - \frac{2}{3}$, as $5\frac{4}{3} - \frac{2}{3}$. Think of $4\frac{1}{10} - \frac{8}{10}$, as $3\frac{11}{10} - \frac{8}{10}$.

17. $3\frac{1}{4} - \frac{2}{4} = $ _____ **18.** $5\frac{3}{6} - \frac{4}{6} = $ _____ **19.** $7\frac{2}{5} - \frac{4}{5} = $ _____

20. $2\frac{2}{10} - \frac{4}{10} = $ _____ **21.** $8\frac{3}{8} - \frac{7}{8} = $ _____ **22.** $1\frac{2}{5} - \frac{3}{5} = $ _____

23. $4\frac{6}{10} - \frac{8}{10} = $ _____ **24.** $3\frac{3}{12} - \frac{5}{12} = $ _____ **25.** $7\frac{1}{3} - \frac{2}{3} = $ _____

26. $6\frac{4}{12}$ **27.** $1\frac{2}{5}$ **28.** $2\frac{3}{6}$
$\quad - \frac{7}{12}$ $\quad - \frac{4}{5}$ $\quad - \frac{5}{6}$
$\overline{\qquad}$ $\overline{\qquad}$ $\overline{\qquad}$

Mentally SUBTRACT:
Use the *same strategy* to rename the mixed numbers below.

29. $6\frac{1}{10} - 2\frac{8}{10} = $ _____ **30.** $12\frac{1}{3} - 5\frac{2}{3} = $ _____ **31.** $5\frac{4}{8} - 2\frac{6}{8} = $ _____

32. $8\frac{2}{6} - 1\frac{3}{6} = $ _____ **33.** $6\frac{5}{12} - 1\frac{7}{12} = $ _____ **34.** $3\frac{2}{10} - 2\frac{6}{10} = $ _____

35. $7\frac{2}{4} - 2\frac{3}{4} = $ _____ **36.** $8\frac{1}{5} - 5\frac{2}{5} = $ _____ **37.** $6\frac{2}{8} - 4\frac{5}{8} = $ _____

38. $3\frac{2}{5}$ **39.** $5\frac{8}{16}$ **40.** $9\frac{3}{5}$
$\quad - 1\frac{4}{5}$ $\quad - 2\frac{10}{16}$ $\quad - 6\frac{4}{5}$
$\overline{\qquad}$ $\overline{\qquad}$ $\overline{\qquad}$

Name _____

Likeable Unlike Fractions

○○○○○○○○○○○○○○○○○○○○○○○○○○○○○○○○○○○○○○○

There are many LIKEABLE UNLIKE FRACTIONS that you can add *mentally*.

Mentally change each fraction to higher terms by thinking of the relationship between the fractions. Write the missing numerator.

1. $\frac{1}{2} = \frac{}{4}$ **2.** $\frac{1}{2} = \frac{}{8}$ **3.** $\frac{1}{2} = \frac{}{6}$ **4.** $\frac{1}{2} = \frac{}{12}$

5. $\frac{1}{3} = \frac{}{6}$ **6.** $\frac{1}{3} = \frac{}{12}$ **7.** $\frac{3}{4} = \frac{}{8}$ **8.** $\frac{1}{4} = \frac{}{12}$

9. $\frac{4}{5} = \frac{}{10}$ **10.** $\frac{3}{4} = \frac{}{12}$ **11.** $\frac{1}{4} = \frac{}{16}$ **12.** $\frac{3}{4} = \frac{}{16}$

The LIKEABLE UNLIKE FRACTIONS are handled *mentally* because the fractions can be made alike easily. Fractions that are related to each other are *quick* and *easy* to use. For example, in $\frac{3}{8} - \frac{1}{4}$, think of $\frac{1}{4}$ as $\frac{2}{8}$, so you have $\frac{3}{8} - \frac{2}{8}$.

13. $\frac{6}{8} - \frac{1}{2} =$ _____   **14.** $\frac{5}{6} - \frac{1}{2} =$ _____   **15.** $\frac{12}{16} - \frac{1}{2} =$ _____

16. $\frac{1}{2} - \frac{2}{6} =$ _____   **17.** $\frac{1}{2} - \frac{5}{12} =$ _____   **18.** $\frac{8}{10} - \frac{3}{5} =$ _____

19. $\frac{1}{3} - \frac{3}{12} =$ _____   **20.** $\frac{3}{4} - \frac{5}{8} =$ _____   **21.** $\frac{3}{8} - \frac{1}{4} =$ _____

22. $\quad \frac{7}{12}$ **23.** $\quad \frac{2}{5}$ **24.** $\quad \frac{4}{6}$ **25.** $\quad \frac{9}{12}$
$\quad\quad - \frac{1}{6}$ $- \frac{3}{10}$ $- \frac{5}{12}$ $- \frac{2}{3}$

26. $\quad \frac{3}{8}$ **27.** $\quad \frac{9}{10}$ **28.** $\quad \frac{15}{16}$ **29** $\quad \frac{3}{4}$
$\quad\quad - \frac{3}{16}$ $- \frac{1}{5}$ $- \frac{3}{4}$ $- \frac{7}{12}$

Mentally subtracting mixed numbers with LIKEABLE UNLIKE FRACTIONS is very similar to what you did above. Only this time, you need to think about the whole number part, too!

30. $3\frac{5}{8} - \frac{1}{2} =$ _____   **31.** $2\frac{6}{8} - \frac{1}{2} =$ _____   **32.** $8\frac{3}{4} - 1\frac{1}{2} =$ _____

33. $5\frac{2}{3} - 1\frac{4}{6} =$ _____   **34.** $6\frac{5}{8} - 1\frac{1}{2} =$ _____   **35.** $7\frac{4}{10} - 3\frac{1}{5} =$ _____

36. $9\frac{4}{8} - 3\frac{1}{4} =$ _____   **37.** $2\frac{3}{6} - 1\frac{1}{3} =$ _____   **38.** $1\frac{9}{10} - 1\frac{1}{2} =$ _____

39. $4\frac{10}{12}$ **40.** $8\frac{6}{16}$ **41.** $3\frac{2}{6}$ **42.** $11\frac{5}{8}$
$\quad - 2\frac{2}{3}$ $- 3\frac{2}{8}$ $- 1\frac{1}{12}$ $- 5\frac{2}{16}$

Name _____

Give Me 1/2 of It

○○○○○○○○○○○○○○○○○○○○○○○○

Taking 1/2 of a number has the same effect as dividing the number by 2.
Find 1/2 of each number.

1. 4 _____   **2.** 10 _____   **3.** 14 _____   **4.** 18 _____

5. 20 _____   **6.** 28 _____   **7.** 32 _____   **8.** 38 _____

9. 40 _____   **10.** 48 _____   **11.** 60¢ _____   **12.** 90¢ _____

13. $1.00 _____   **14.** 300 _____   **15.** 500 _____   **16.** 800 _____

17. 1,200 _____   **18.** 1,480 _____   **19.** 2,638 _____   **20.** 2.48 _____

21. 16.028 _____ **22.** 30 _____   **23.** 70 _____   **24.** 90 _____

25. 130 _____   **26.** 150 _____   **27.** 25 _____   **28.** 75 _____

29. 83 _____   **30.** 99 _____   **31.** $\frac{1}{2}$ _____   **32.** $\frac{1}{8}$ _____

33. $\frac{1}{3}$ _____   **34.** $\frac{4}{6}$ _____   **35.** $\frac{1}{5}$ _____   **36.** $\frac{2}{7}$ _____

37. $4\frac{1}{3}$ _____   **38.** $6\frac{1}{3}$ _____   **39.** $10\frac{1}{4}$ _____   **40.** $15\frac{1}{2}$ _____

Now that you can find 1/2 of a number, you're ready to find other fractional parts of numbers *mentally*. Use the same division thinking pattern that you used above.

FIND 1/4 OF:

41. 32 _____   **42.** 1.20 _____   **43.** 40 _____   **44.** 1.60 _____   **45.** 60 _____

46. 2.00 _____ **47.** 80 _____   **48.** 2.40 _____ **49.** 100 _____   **50.** 30.0 _____

FIND 1/3 OF:

51. 15 _____   **52.** 1.50 _____   **53.** 45 _____   **54.** 1.80 _____   **55.** 60 _____

56. 3.00 _____ **57.** 75 _____   **58.** 33.3 _____ **59.** 90 _____   **60.** 3.60 _____

FIND 1/5 OF:

61. 3.5 _____   **62.** 12.5 _____   **63.** 5.0 _____   **64.** 2.55 _____   **65.** 5.5 _____

66. 3.10 _____ **67.** 7.5 _____   **68.** 55.5 _____ **69.** 100 _____   **70.** 6.05 _____

Name _____

Quick Fraction Multiplication

In an earlier fraction activity, *Give Me 1/2 of It*, you found a fractional part of a number. You can use this skill to find *mentally* more than a simple fractional part of a number.

Read to find out what students in one class did.

TEACHER: A quick review shows us that we easily found that $\frac{1}{4}$ of 20 is 5. We divided 20 by 4; $20 \div 4$ equals 5.
If $\frac{1}{4}$ of 20 is 5, then how much is $\frac{2}{4}$ of 20?

ANNETTE: It is twice or two times the answer for $\frac{1}{4}$ of 20. So $\frac{2}{4}$ of 20 is 2 times $\frac{1}{4}$ of 20, or 2 x 5, or 10.

TEACHER: Then, what is $\frac{3}{4}$ of 20?

ANNETTE: If $\frac{1}{4}$ of 20 is 5, then $\frac{3}{4}$ of 20 is 3 times the 5, or 15.

TEACHER: Good thinking, Annette.

Using the same thinking pattern as Annette did, solve the following.

1. $\frac{2}{3} \times 6 =$ _____

2. $\frac{3}{4} \times 12 =$ _____

3. $\frac{5}{6}$ of 18 = _____

4. $\frac{2}{5}$ of 10 = _____

5. $\frac{6}{10}$ of 30 = _____

6. $\frac{3}{5} \times 40 =$ _____

7. $\frac{2}{8} \times 16 =$ _____

8. $\frac{3}{4} \times 28 =$ _____

9. $\frac{4}{5}$ of 25 = _____

10. $\frac{4}{6}$ of 30 = _____

11. $\frac{3}{10} \times 40 =$ _____

12. $\frac{3}{8} \times 32 =$ _____

13. $\frac{5}{6} \times 42 =$ _____

14. $\frac{2}{3}$ of 33 = _____

15. $\frac{5}{6} \times 36 =$ _____

16. $\frac{5}{12} \times 24 =$ _____

17. $\frac{7}{8} \times 40 =$ _____

18. $\frac{2}{9} \times 27 =$ _____

19. $\frac{4}{7}$ of 14 = _____

20. $\frac{7}{16} \times 48 =$ _____

21. $\frac{4}{10} \times 120 =$ _____

22. $\frac{5}{8} \times 80 =$ _____

23. $\frac{3}{4}$ of 200 = _____

24. $\frac{7}{12} \times 360 =$ _____

25. $\frac{7}{8} \times 400 =$ _____

26. $1\frac{2}{3}$ of 12 = _____

27. $\frac{3}{4} \times 84 =$ _____

28. $1\frac{3}{8} \times 24 =$ _____

29. $2\frac{2}{3} \times 6 =$ _____

30. $1\frac{4}{6} \times 18 =$ _____

Name _____

Proportions

○ ○ ○ ○ ○ ○ ○ ○ ○ ○ ○ ○ ○ ○ ○ ○ ○ ○

Look at the examples below. Would you believe that *mentally* you can find x, the unknown? Yes, you really can! You don't need to cross multiply, either!

$$\frac{x}{64} = \frac{7}{8} \qquad\qquad \frac{45}{x} = \frac{9}{4} \qquad\qquad \frac{25}{3} = \frac{x}{6} \qquad\qquad \frac{12}{2} = \frac{120}{x}$$

You use the same technique you use when changing fractions to higher or lower terms. You are either multiplying or dividing both terms by the same number. Remember the Golden Rule of Fractions?

Write the missing numerator or denominator.

1. $\frac{1}{2} = \frac{}{4}$ 2. $\frac{2}{3} = \frac{4}{}$ 3. $\frac{}{} = \frac{6}{8}$ 4. $\frac{}{10} = \frac{1}{2}$

5. $\frac{4}{5} = \frac{12}{}$ 6. $\frac{5}{} = \frac{10}{16}$ 7. $\frac{}{7} = \frac{9}{21}$ 8. $\frac{15}{20} = \frac{}{4}$

9. $\frac{1}{} = \frac{12}{24}$ 10. $\frac{2}{} = \frac{16}{24}$ 11. $\frac{25}{} = \frac{1}{3}$ 12. $\frac{27}{45} = \frac{3}{}$

13. $\frac{}{64} = \frac{4}{8}$ 14. $\frac{60}{100} = \frac{}{5}$ 15. $\frac{17}{} = \frac{1}{3}$ 16. $\frac{8}{10} = \frac{16}{}$

17. $\frac{15}{40} = \frac{}{8}$ 18. $\frac{}{66} = \frac{3}{6}$ 19. $\frac{2}{} = \frac{28}{42}$ 20. $\frac{7}{9} = \frac{}{63}$

21. $\frac{56}{} = \frac{7}{2}$ 22. $\frac{39}{13} = \frac{}{1}$ 23. $\frac{7}{2} = \frac{35}{}$ 24. $\frac{}{15} = \frac{90}{30}$

25. $\frac{6}{} = \frac{48}{8}$ 26. $\frac{80}{} = \frac{4}{3}$ 27. $\frac{64}{24} = \frac{}{3}$ 28. $\frac{13}{12} = \frac{}{60}$

Division Strategies

Read the strategies below to help you understand how to divide the examples in the box *mentally*.

$$\frac{3}{4} \div \frac{1}{4} = \qquad\qquad \frac{8}{10} \div \frac{2}{10} = \qquad\qquad 1 \div \frac{1}{6} =$$

STRATEGY 1

To solve these examples, you DO NOT need to change the sign and multiply by the reciprocal. Instead, picture what's being asked. For example, in $\frac{3}{4} \div \frac{1}{4}$, picture a drawing to help you.

$\frac{3}{4}$

Now, how many ◢ ($\frac{1}{4}$) are contained in $\frac{3}{4}$?
Can you see that the answer is 3?

✱ In $\frac{8}{10} \div \frac{2}{10}$, you need to **picture** how many groups of $\frac{2}{10}$ are contained in $\frac{8}{10}$.

There are 4 groups of $\frac{2}{10}$ in $\frac{8}{10}$.

✱ In $1 \div \frac{1}{6}$, you need to picture how many $\frac{1}{6}$ are contained in 1 whole. There are 6 ($\frac{1}{6}$) in one whole!

STRATEGY 2

Another way to think about $\frac{3}{4} \div \frac{1}{4}$ is to think of it as you would whole number division, such as $6 \div 2$ or $2\overline{)6}$.

Think of $\frac{3}{4} \div \frac{1}{4}$ as $\frac{1}{4}\overline{)\frac{3}{4}}$. There are 3 ($\frac{1}{4}$) in $\frac{3}{4}$.

When $\frac{3}{4} \div \frac{1}{4}$ is thought of as $\frac{1}{4}\overline{)\frac{3}{4}}$, you are less inclined to try the reciprocal method for division. Instead, it makes the example easy to *understand* and *solve* mentally.

$\frac{8}{10} \div \frac{2}{10}$ Think $\frac{2}{10}\overline{)\frac{8}{10}}$ There are 4 ($\frac{2}{10}$) in $\frac{8}{10}$.
$\longrightarrow$

$1 \div \frac{1}{6}$ Think $\frac{1}{6}\overline{)1}$.   There are 6 ($\frac{1}{6}$) in one whole.
$\longrightarrow$

61

Name _____

Using Division Strategies

Solve the division below *mentally*. Don't forget the strategies you've learned.

1. $\frac{2}{3} \div \frac{1}{3} =$ _____

2. $\frac{2}{4} \div \frac{1}{4} =$ _____

3. $\frac{5}{6} \div \frac{1}{6} =$ _____

4. $\frac{6}{8} \div \frac{1}{8} =$ _____

5. $\frac{7}{10} \div \frac{1}{10} =$ _____

6. $\frac{6}{12} \div \frac{1}{12} =$ _____

7. $\frac{14}{16} \div \frac{1}{16} =$ _____

8. $\frac{2}{3} \div \frac{2}{3} =$ _____

9. $\frac{4}{6} \div \frac{2}{6} =$ _____

10. $\frac{6}{10} \div \frac{2}{10} =$ _____

11. $\frac{6}{12} \div \frac{3}{12} =$ _____

12. $\frac{8}{16} \div \frac{4}{16} =$ _____

13. $\frac{6}{8} \div \frac{2}{8} =$ _____

14. $\frac{8}{10} \div \frac{4}{10} =$ _____

15. $\frac{6}{8} \div \frac{3}{8} =$ _____

16. $1 \div \frac{1}{4} =$ _____

17. $1 \div \frac{4}{16} =$ _____

18. $1 \div \frac{2}{8} =$ _____

19. $1 \div \frac{2}{10} =$ _____

20. $1 \div \frac{4}{8} =$ _____

21. $\frac{7}{8} \div \frac{1}{8} =$ _____

22. $\frac{8}{12} \div \frac{4}{12} =$ _____

23. $1 \div \frac{1}{2} =$ _____

24. $2 \div \frac{1}{2} =$ _____

25. $3 \div \frac{1}{2} =$ _____

26. $1 \div \frac{1}{4} =$ _____

27. $2 \div \frac{1}{4} =$ _____

28. $3 \div \frac{1}{4} =$ _____

29. $2 \div \frac{2}{8} =$ _____

30. $3 \div \frac{2}{8} =$ _____

31. $4 \div \frac{1}{10} =$ _____

32. $4 \div \frac{2}{10} =$ _____

33. $4 \div \frac{5}{10} =$ _____

34. $2 \div \frac{2}{3} =$ _____

35. $2 \div \frac{1}{5} =$ _____

36. $6 \div \frac{1}{3} =$ _____

37. $6 \div \frac{1}{4} =$ _____

38. $7 \div \frac{1}{5} =$ _____

39. $8 \div \frac{1}{6} =$ _____

40. $10 \div \frac{1}{2} =$ _____

41. $1\frac{1}{2} \div \frac{1}{2} =$ _____

42. $1\frac{3}{4} \div \frac{1}{4} =$ _____

43. $2\frac{1}{2} \div \frac{1}{2} =$ _____

44. $2\frac{1}{4} \div \frac{1}{4} =$ _____

45. $3\frac{2}{5} \div \frac{1}{5} =$ _____

46. $1\frac{6}{8} \div \frac{1}{8} =$ _____

47. $1\frac{6}{8} \div \frac{2}{8} =$ _____

48. $1\frac{4}{8} \div \frac{4}{8} =$ _____

49. $2\frac{4}{6} \div \frac{2}{6} =$ _____

50. $2\frac{3}{6} \div \frac{3}{6} =$ _____

51. $2\frac{1}{3} \div \frac{1}{3} =$ _____

52. $1\frac{4}{5} \div \frac{1}{5} =$ _____

53. $3\frac{6}{10} \div \frac{1}{10} =$ _____

54. $4\frac{6}{10} \div \frac{2}{10} =$ _____

Name _____

Using Equivalent Fractions:
STILL HARDER DIVISION DONE MENTALLY

You also can divide these *mentally*: $\frac{1}{2} \div \frac{2}{16}$, $3\frac{1}{5} \div \frac{2}{10}$, $6\frac{2}{4} \div \frac{8}{16}$.
How? Keep in mind the two strategies you learned earlier:

* ✳ Picture what is being asked.

* ✳ Think of fraction division as: $\overline{)}$.

Now it's time for a new strategy.

Think of equivalent fractions!

Remember that $\frac{2}{8} = \frac{1}{4}$, $\frac{1}{2} = \frac{3}{6}$, $\frac{2}{10} = \frac{1}{5}$, and so on.

* ✳ When you see $\frac{1}{4} \div \frac{1}{8}$, remember that there are 2 $(\frac{1}{8})$ equal to $\frac{1}{4}$.

* ✳ In $\frac{1}{2} \div \frac{1}{6}$, you know that $\frac{3}{6} = \frac{1}{2}$, so the answer is 3.
  There are 3 $(\frac{1}{6})$ in $\frac{1}{2}$.

* ✳ In $\frac{4}{10} \div \frac{1}{5}$, you know that $\frac{2}{10} = \frac{1}{5}$, so the answer is 20.
  There are 2 $(\frac{1}{5})$ in $\frac{4}{10}$.

You may also rename one and/or both fractions.

In $\frac{8}{12} \div \frac{2}{6}$ we can rename one fraction:

* ✳ $\frac{8}{12} = \frac{4}{6}$, so in $\frac{8}{12} \div \frac{2}{6}$ we now have $\frac{4}{6} \div \frac{2}{6} = 2$.

or

* ✳ $\frac{2}{6} = \frac{4}{12}$, so in $\frac{8}{12} \div \frac{2}{6}$ we now have $\frac{8}{12} \div \frac{4}{12} = 2$.

In $\frac{4}{8} \div \frac{6}{12}$ we can rename both fractions:

* ✳ $\frac{4}{8} = \frac{1}{2}$ and $\frac{6}{12} = \frac{1}{2}$, so in $\frac{4}{8} \div \frac{6}{12}$ we now have $\frac{1}{2} \div \frac{1}{2} = 1$.

63

Name _____

Still Harder Division Done Mentally Using Equivalent Fractions

Use the new strategy from the USING EQUIVALENT FRACTIONS on page 63 to find the answer *mentally*.

Remember when using equivalents that one whole can equal $\frac{2}{2}$, $\frac{3}{3}$, $\frac{4}{4}$, or one whole can equal 3 groups of $\frac{2}{6}$ or 3 ($\frac{2}{6}$), 5 groups of $\frac{2}{10}$ or 5 ($\frac{2}{10}$), 2 groups of $\frac{5}{10}$ or 2 ($\frac{5}{10}$), and so on.

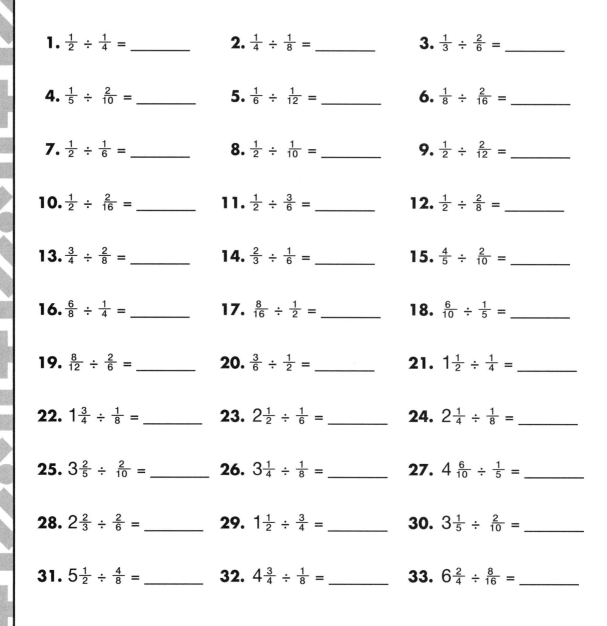

1. $\frac{1}{2} \div \frac{1}{4} =$ _____

2. $\frac{1}{4} \div \frac{1}{8} =$ _____

3. $\frac{1}{3} \div \frac{2}{6} =$ _____

4. $\frac{1}{5} \div \frac{2}{10} =$ _____

5. $\frac{1}{6} \div \frac{1}{12} =$ _____

6. $\frac{1}{8} \div \frac{2}{16} =$ _____

7. $\frac{1}{2} \div \frac{1}{6} =$ _____

8. $\frac{1}{2} \div \frac{1}{10} =$ _____

9. $\frac{1}{2} \div \frac{2}{12} =$ _____

10. $\frac{1}{2} \div \frac{2}{16} =$ _____

11. $\frac{1}{2} \div \frac{3}{6} =$ _____

12. $\frac{1}{2} \div \frac{2}{8} =$ _____

13. $\frac{3}{4} \div \frac{2}{8} =$ _____

14. $\frac{2}{3} \div \frac{1}{6} =$ _____

15. $\frac{4}{5} \div \frac{2}{10} =$ _____

16. $\frac{6}{8} \div \frac{1}{4} =$ _____

17. $\frac{8}{16} \div \frac{1}{2} =$ _____

18. $\frac{6}{10} \div \frac{1}{5} =$ _____

19. $\frac{8}{12} \div \frac{2}{6} =$ _____

20. $\frac{3}{6} \div \frac{1}{2} =$ _____

21. $1\frac{1}{2} \div \frac{1}{4} =$ _____

22. $1\frac{3}{4} \div \frac{1}{8} =$ _____

23. $2\frac{1}{2} \div \frac{1}{6} =$ _____

24. $2\frac{1}{4} \div \frac{1}{8} =$ _____

25. $3\frac{2}{5} \div \frac{2}{10} =$ _____

26. $3\frac{1}{4} \div \frac{1}{8} =$ _____

27. $4\frac{6}{10} \div \frac{1}{5} =$ _____

28. $2\frac{2}{3} \div \frac{2}{6} =$ _____

29. $1\frac{1}{2} \div \frac{3}{4} =$ _____

30. $3\frac{1}{5} \div \frac{2}{10} =$ _____

31. $5\frac{1}{2} \div \frac{4}{8} =$ _____

32. $4\frac{3}{4} \div \frac{1}{8} =$ _____

33. $6\frac{2}{4} \div \frac{8}{16} =$ _____

USING MENTAL COMPUTATION WITH DECIMALS

Many of the worksheets are self-explanatory, however, you are strongly encouraged to:

* be liberal in your use of overheads as a basis for examples, or write examples on the board for the class to discuss.

* stress the similarities between operations with decimals and operations with whole numbers.

* stress the use of number facts, especially in division.

* stress the movement of the decimal point when multiplying or dividing by powers of 10.

$$4.2 \times 10 = 42 \qquad 4.2 \times .1 = .42$$
$$4.2 \div 10 = .42 \qquad 4.2 \div .1 = 42$$

Discuss which powers of 10 give larger numbers and why. Also, talk about when the decimal point should be moved to the *right* and to the *left*.

* stress the visual movement of the decimal point in the dividend.

$$.3 \overline{).1\,2} \qquad 3.\overline{)1.2} \qquad .004 \overline{)1.2} \qquad 4.\overline{)1200.}$$

* stress the need for zeroes either to even out an answer or to fulfill the place value requirements of an operation.

$$.4 \overline{).10} \qquad .3 \times .2 = .06 \qquad 3.4 \div 100 = .034$$

* study the bottom of page 82 under **USING FRACTIONAL EQUIVALENTS AND ROLE REVERSAL** for mentally computing with decimals that can be changed easily to fractions.

$.30 \times 20 =$	$.6$ of $35 =$	$.33\frac{1}{3} \times 18 =$	$.12 \times 75 =$
$\frac{3}{10} \times 20 =$	$\frac{6}{10}$ of $35 =$	$\frac{1}{3} \times 18 =$	$12 \times .75 =$
6	21	6	$12 \times \frac{3}{4} =$
			9

Name _____

Mentally Adding Tenths

Add the center decimal to each decimal around it. Write the answer on the line in the connecting empty circle. *The strategy is to think the renaming or carrying step.*

EXAMPLE: 9.7 + .5   **1.** .7 + .5 = 1.2   **2.** Increase 9 by 1.   **3.** The answer is 10.2.
                      Think .2   9 → 10

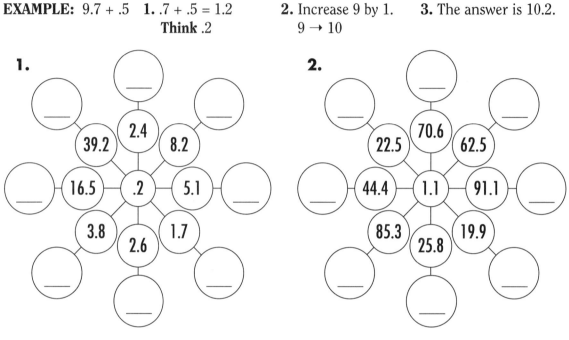

1.

39.2   2.4   8.2
16.5   .2   5.1
3.8   2.6   1.7

2.

22.5   70.6   62.5
44.4   1.1   91.1
85.3   25.8   19.9

The strategy below deals only with the tenths places in both decimals.

EXAMPLE: .9 + 5.83
   1. .9 + .8 = 1.7   **2.** Increase the 5 by 1.   **3.** The answer is 6.73.
   Think .7   5 → 6
   Adding .9 has no affect on the decimal places to the right of the tenths.

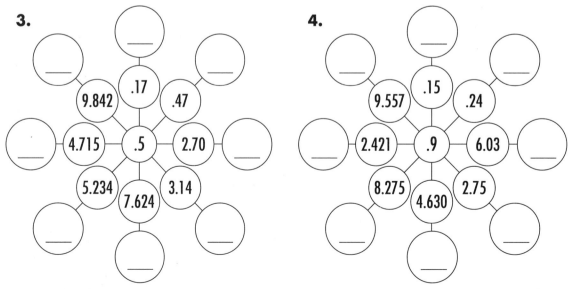

3.

9.842   .17   .47
4.715   .5   2.70
5.234   7.624   3.14

4.

9.557   .15   .24
2.421   .9   6.03
8.275   4.630   2.75

Name _____

Counting Forward by Decimals

○○○

Count forward by the number given at the left of each row. The number with which you begin counting is given.

Remember the *strategy* is to **THINK** the addition by adding the same decimal places and automatically taking care of any renaming or carrying. See the example below.

> .2 + 3.9 **THINK** .2 + .9 yields a .1.   Increase the 3 by 1.

		.7,	.9,	1.1,	1.3,	1.5,	1.7.
	.2						
1.	**.3**	.2,	____,	____,	____,	____,	____.
2.	**.4**	1.3,	____,	____,	____,	____,	____.
3.	**.5**	1.4,	____,	____,	____,	____,	____.
4.	**.6**	3.4,	____,	____,	____,	____,	____.
5.	**.7**	5.8,	____,	____,	____,	____,	____.
6.	**.8**	4.3,	____,	____,	____,	____,	____.
7.	**.9**	2.1,	____,	____,	____,	____,	____.

Mentally Adding Hundredths and Thousandths

○ ○

Add the decimal at the beginning of each line to each decimal to the right. Write the answer on the line below.

1. .2	.35	.463	2.545	5.4	7.863
	_____	_____	_____	_____	_____
2. .002	.391	6.2077	5.3567	2.939	2.460
	_____	_____	_____	_____	_____
3. .05	.623	9.718	3.2763	8.4043	.6853
	_____	_____	_____	_____	_____
4. .005	2.967	7.766	4.833	2.397	.6853
	_____	_____	_____	_____	_____
5. .09	.006	1.04	2.111	4.583	9.921
	_____	_____	_____	_____	_____
6. .009	3.157	.4245	6.408	3.3556	1.7281
	_____	_____	_____	_____	_____

Name _____

Counting Backward by Decimals

ooooooooooooooooooooooooooooooooooooooooooo

Count backwards by the number given. The number with which you begin counting backwards is given.

The strategy is to **THINK** *the subtraction by subtracting the endings and automatically taking care of any renaming or borrowing. See the example below.*

6.3 - .4   **THINK** .4 from 1.3 yields .9.   The 6 becomes 1 less, or 5.

EXAMPLE: Count backwards by .2:
5.8, 5.6, 5.4, 5.2, 5.0, 4.8, 4.6, 4.4, 4.2, 4.0, 3.8, 3.6

1. Count backwards by .3:

7.0, _____, _____, _____, _____, _____, _____, _____, _____, _____, _____, _____

2. Count backwards by .4:

4.7, _____, _____, _____, _____, _____, _____, _____, _____, _____, _____, _____

3. Count backwards by .5:

9.3, _____, _____, _____, _____, _____, _____, _____, _____, _____, _____, _____

4. Count backwards by .6:

8.7, _____, _____, _____, _____, _____, _____, _____, _____, _____, _____, _____

5. Count backwards by .7:

15.3, _____, _____, _____, _____, _____, _____, _____, _____, _____, _____, _____

6. Count backwards by .8:

20.5, _____, _____, _____, _____, _____, _____, _____, _____, _____, _____, _____

7. Count backwards by .9:

19.1, _____, _____, _____, _____, _____, _____, _____, _____, _____, _____, _____

Using Money to Subtract Decimals Mentally

○ ○

Our money system is a decimal system. THINK of subtracting decimals as you would THINK of subtracting money *mentally*. The subtraction is much *easier without* resorting to borrowing or renaming.

EXAMPLE: 5 - 1.75 **Think** $5.00 - $1.75.
　　　　　　　→

Subtract the decimal from the number in the IN column.
Write the answer in the OUT column.

1.

Subtract .25

IN	OUT
.75	.50
1.50	1.25
3.50	
4.75	
5.00	
6.25	
4.35	
3.40	

2.

Subtract .50

IN	OUT
5	
4.25	
3.75	
6.5	
7.0	
6.6	
4.80	
3.65	

3.

Subtract 1.50

IN	OUT
10	
4	
3	
2.75	
4.25	
5.50	
1.6	
2.8	

4.

Subtract .75

IN	OUT
1.00	
2.0	
3.75	
4.50	
1.25	
6.80	
3.90	
2.86	

Name _____

Instant Decimal Subtraction

You will be able to do the following more quickly than you think.

1 - .476   10 - 6.573

```
  10.000        1.0000      100.00000
-  6.287      -  .4683     -  34.67892
```

* Review **INSTANT SUBTRACTION** of whole numbers on page 36. The same principles apply to decimals.

* Remember complements? Each digit in the answer is derived by adding the digit to be subtracted to "some" number that gives you 9. The exception is the digit furthest to the right. It must be added to "some" number to get 10.

The examples below will refresh your memory.

1 - .437 = ?   Change to the following form:
```
  1.000
-  .437
```

The answer is: 4 + ? = 9
```
               3 + ? = 9        1.000
               7 + ? = 10     -  .437
                                .563
```

Subtract the decimals below using your newly learned *quick* method.
NOTE: In   10.000   notice where you need to end thinking 9 and begin 10.
```
          -  5.440
```

1. 1.00   **2.** 1.000   **3.** 1.   **4.** 10.
```
     - .38            -  .826           - .351           - 4.7
```

5. 10.00   **6.** 10.000   **7.** 10.   **8.** 100.0
```
     - 5.13           - 2.924           - 6.4324          - 37.4278
```

9. 10 - 3.7245 = _____   **10.** 100 - 76.44821 = _____

11. 10.000   **12.** 1.0000   **13.** 100.00   **14.** 1,000.0
```
      - 7.360           - 5610            - 83.40           - 620.0
```

Name _____

Subtracting Decimal Cards

Below are eight decimal cards. Choose the pair of cards that will give the answer when you mentally subtract them. Use the strategy or strategies that seem easiest to you. Write your answers in the boxes.

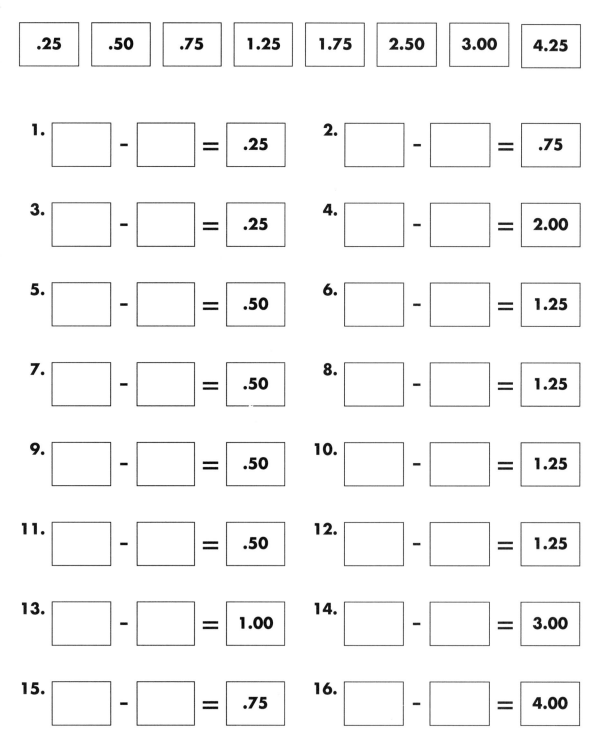

| .25 | .50 | .75 | 1.25 | 1.75 | 2.50 | 3.00 | 4.25 |

1. ☐ - ☐ = .25

2. ☐ - ☐ = .75

3. ☐ - ☐ = .25

4. ☐ - ☐ = 2.00

5. ☐ - ☐ = .50

6. ☐ - ☐ = 1.25

7. ☐ - ☐ = .50

8. ☐ - ☐ = 1.25

9. ☐ - ☐ = .50

10. ☐ - ☐ = 1.25

11. ☐ - ☐ = .50

12. ☐ - ☐ = 1.25

13. ☐ - ☐ = 1.00

14. ☐ - ☐ = 3.00

15. ☐ - ☐ = .75

16. ☐ - ☐ = 4.00

Name _____

Multiplying Decimals by 10, 100, and 1,000

○○○○○○○○○○○○○○○○○○○○○○○○○○○○○○○○○

Look at the examples below. Do you see a pattern?

10 x .6 = 6	10 x 2.4 = 24	10 x 45.136 = 451.36
100 x .6 = 60	100 x 2.4 = 240	100 x 45.136 = 4,513.6
1,000 x .6 = 600	1,000 x 2.4 = 2,400	1,000 x 45.136 = 45,136

Did you notice that multiplying:

✱ by 10 moved the decimal point one place to the right?

✱ by 100 moved the decimal point two places to the right?

✱ by 1,000 moved the decimal point three places to the right?

The rule is simple: *Move the decimal point to the right for each zero in 10, 100, or 1,000.*

Fill in the space below with 10, 100, or 1,000 to make true equations.

1. .3 x _____ = 3

2. _____ x .14 = 1.4

3. .25 x _____ = 250

4. 3.7 x _____ = 37

5. .92 x _____ = 92

6. _____ x 1.17 = 11.7

7. _____ x 3.9 = 390

8. _____ x 26.133 = 2,613.3

9. 123.050 x _____ = 1,230.5

10. _____ x .687 = 687

11. _____ x 23.005 = 2,300.5

12. _____ x 87.2314 = 872.314

Multiply *mentally.*

13. 10 x 3.24 = _____

14. 4.5 x 10 = _____

15. 100 x .67 = _____

16. 5.12 x 1,000 = _____

17. 399.7 x 1,000 = _____

18. .621 x 1,000 = _____

19. .008 x 10 = _____

20. .9210 x 1,000 = _____

21. 100 x 7.6215 = _____

22. 983.0 x 100 = _____

23. 1,000 x .4563 = _____

24. 10 x .9114 = _____

25. 10 x .01 = _____

26. 10 x .0110 = _____

27. 1,000 x .01447 = _____

28. 1,000 x .1 = _____

29. 100 x .43 = _____

30. 100 x .45 = _____

Name _____

Multiplying Decimals by .1, .01, and .001

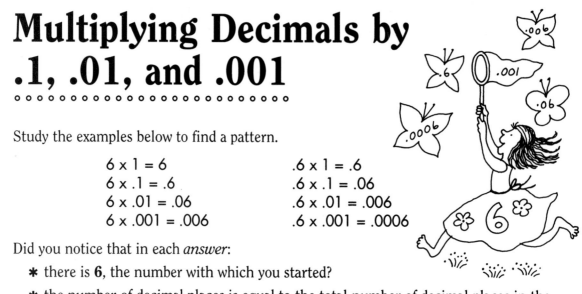

○ ○

Study the examples below to find a pattern.

6 x 1 = 6	.6 x 1 = .6
6 x .1 = .6	.6 x .1 = .06
6 x .01 = .06	.6 x .01 = .006
6 x .001 = .006	.6 x .001 = .0006

Did you notice that in each *answer*:

* there is **6**, the number with which you started?
* the number of decimal places is equal to the total number of decimal places in the two factors?

Do the following multiplication *mentally*:

1. 7 x .1 = _____   **2.** 9 x .01 = _____

3. .9 x .1 = _____   **4.** 2.5 x .1 = _____

5. 2.5 x .01 = _____   **6.** .23 x .01 = _____

7. .23 x .001 = _____   **8.** .415 x .01 = _____

9. 41.5 x .01 = _____   **10.** 415 x .01 = _____

11. .1 x .1 = _____   **12.** .01 x .1 = _____

13. .01 x .01 = _____   **14.** .001 x .01 = _____

15. .001 x .001 = _____   **16.** .0001 x .35 = _____

17. .01 x .006 = _____   **18.** .0023 x .1 = _____

19. .004 x .2 = _____   **20.** .005 x .02 = _____

21. .01 x .03 x .02 = _____   **22.** .06 x .007 x .01 = _____

23. .45 x .02 = _____   **24.** 3.25 x .03 = _____

What Decimal Are You Calling?

DIRECTIONS: Cut out and distribute to students. A student reads her or his card. The student who has the correct number on her or his card should answer. The game continues until the first card is repeated.

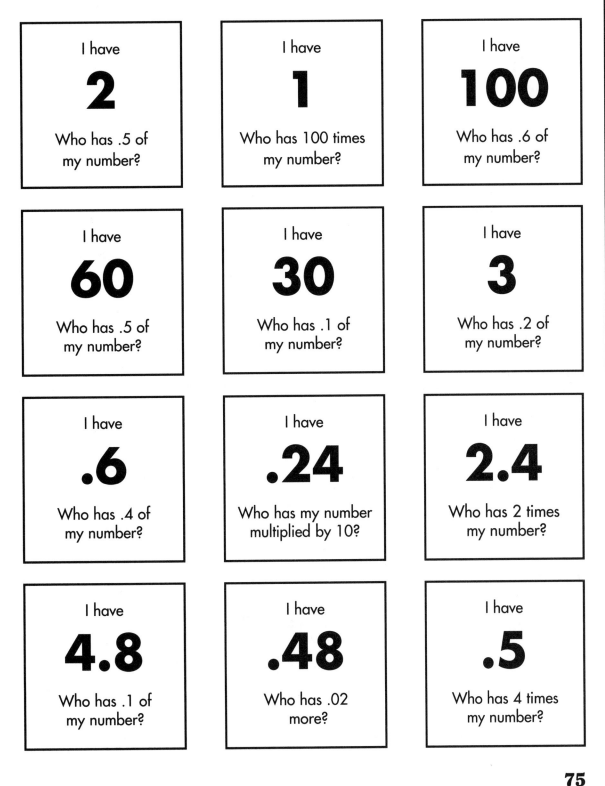

I have
2
Who has .5 of
my number?

I have
1
Who has 100 times
my number?

I have
100
Who has .6 of
my number?

I have
60
Who has .5 of
my number?

I have
30
Who has .1 of
my number?

I have
3
Who has .2 of
my number?

I have
.6
Who has .4 of
my number?

I have
.24
Who has my number
multiplied by 10?

I have
2.4
Who has 2 times
my number?

I have
4.8
Who has .1 of
my number?

I have
.48
Who has .02
more?

I have
.5
Who has 4 times
my number?

Name _____

Dividing Decimals by 10, 100, and 1,000

o o o o o o o o o o o o o o o o o o o o o o o o o o o o o o o o

Being able to divide a decimal by 10, 100, and 1,000 *mentally* is an extremely valuable skill to have. You'll soon see how really easy it is to divide decimals by these numbers.

To learn this easy strategy, watch what happens to the decimal point in the examples below.

$$24.6 \div 10 = 2\,.\,4\,.\,6$$
$$24.6 \div 100 = .2\,4\,.\,6$$
$$24.6 \div 1,000 = .024.6$$

STRATEGY: *The decimal point is moved as many places to the LEFT as there are zeroes in the 10's, 100's, or 1,000's .*

Notice that the answers are smaller because you are dividing by a whole number. Also, notice that dividing by 10 is the same as multiplying by $\frac{1}{10}$. Dividing by 100 is the same as multiplying by $\frac{1}{100}$. Dividing by 1,000 is the same as multiplying by $\frac{1}{1000}$.

Use your new strategy to divide mentally.

1. $364 \div 10 =$ _____

2. $364 \div 100 =$ _____

3. $364 \div 1,000 =$ _____

4. $25.48 \div 10 =$ _____

5. $25.48 \div 100 =$ _____

6. $25.48 \div 1,000 =$ _____

7. $1.85 \div 10 =$ _____

8. $46.4 \div 100 =$ _____

9. $5.13 \div 1,000 =$ _____

10. $.5 \div 10 =$ _____

11. $4.33 \div 100 =$ _____

12. $\$1.10 \div 10 =$ _____

13. $12.6 \div 1,000 =$ _____

14. $8.37 \div 100 =$ _____

15. $\$128.00 \div 100 =$ _____

16. $8,634 \div 1,000 =$ _____

17. $489.7 \div 10 =$ _____

18. $556.8 \div 1,000 =$ _____

19. $\$2,867.00 \div 100 =$ _____

20. $89 \div 100 =$ _____

21. $\$9,860.00 \div 1,000 =$ _____

22. $9.8 \div 100 =$ _____

76

Name _____

Dividing Decimals by .1, .01, and .001

To learn a *quick* and *easy* strategy for dividing by .1, .01, and .001, look at the examples below. Observe the movement of the decimal point.

$$5.23 \div .1 = 52.3$$
$$5.23 \div .01 = 523.0$$
$$5.23 \div .001 = 5230.0$$

STRATEGY: *The decimal point is moved to the RIGHT as many decimal places as there are in .1, .01, .001.*

Notice that the answers are larger because you are dividing by a smaller quantity. Also, notice that dividing by .1 is the same as multiplying by 10. Dividing by .01 is the same as multiplying by 100. Dividing by .001 is the same as multiplying by 1,000.

Use your new strategy to divide *mentally.*

1. 1.84 ÷ .1 = _____

2. 1.84 ÷ .01 = _____

3. 1.84 ÷ .001 = _____

4. 34.7 ÷ .1 = _____

5. 34.7 ÷ .01 = _____

6. 34.7 ÷ .001 = _____

7. 458 ÷ .1 = _____

8. 458 ÷ .01 = _____

9. 458 ÷ .001 = _____

10. 36 ÷ .1 = _____

11. 4.8 ÷ .01 = _____

12. 367.2 ÷ .10 = _____

13. 8.84 ÷ .001 = _____

14. .96 ÷ .01 = _____

15. .230 ÷ .001 = _____

16. .45 ÷ .10 = _____

17. .78 ÷ .01 = _____

18. 2.46 ÷ .01 = _____

19. 3.42 ÷ .001 = _____

20. .05 ÷ .01 = _____

21. .4 ÷ .1 = _____

22. .036 ÷ .001 = _____

23. 14.1 ÷ .01 = _____

24. 6 ÷ .1 = _____

77

Decimal Division with a Potpourri of Strategies

o o o o o o o o o o o o o o o o o o o o o o o o o o o o o o o o o o o o o o o

Mentally dividing a decimal by a *whole number* and dividing a decimal by a *decimal* involves **A POTPOURRI OF STRATEGIES**.

Here are some strategies to keep in mind:

> ✳ *Look for number facts:* $3\overline{)1.2}$, $6\overline{)1.8}$, $.6\overline{)3.6}$

> ✳ *Think about where the decimal points are placed.*
>
>   in the dividend: $.7.\overline{).2.1}$, $.05.\overline{).25.5}$
>
>   in the quotient: $6\overline{)1.2}$, $4\overline{).016}$

> ✳ *Think about where the zeroes are placed.*
>
>   in the dividend: $.08\overline{)1.6}$
>
>   in the dividend to even out an answer: $5\overline{)1.4\underline{0}}$
>
>   in the quotient: $4\overline{).16}$

Mentally compute the answers to the decimal division below. Use your strategies.

1. $5\overline{)4.5}$ **2.** $6\overline{).36}$ **3.** $7\overline{).420}$ **4.** $3\overline{).021}$ **5.** $4\overline{)8.044}$

6. $5\overline{)5.010}$ **7.** $2\overline{)4.0012}$ **8.** $5\overline{)1.4}$ **9.** $4\overline{).02}$ **10.** $20\overline{)4.0}$

11. $80\overline{)6.40}$ **12.** $90\overline{).72}$ **13.** $30\overline{)6.030}$ **14.** $50\overline{)15.0}$ **15.** $.7\overline{)2.1}$

16. $.7\overline{).21}$ **17.** $.07\overline{).21}$ **18.** $.08\overline{).32}$ **19.** $.08\overline{)3.2}$ **20.** $.8\overline{).32}$

21. $.6\overline{)4.2}$ **22.** $.7\overline{).49}$ **23.** $.07\overline{).56}$ **24.** $.07\overline{)3.5}$ **25.** $.3\overline{)1.8}$

26. $.9\overline{).018}$ **27.** $.4\overline{).0404}$ **28.** $2.5\overline{)5}$ **29.** $.14\overline{)2.8}$ **30.** $.1.8\overline{)3.6}$

The first thing you need to do is to become familiar with the *tasks* and *mental* requirements of the worksheets in this section. You will need to stress discussions, pupil thinking, and understanding **before** worksheets are assigned.

Stress the following:

∗ Fractions can make percents easy to handle.

∗ Changing percents to lower-term fractions is an important and easy skill to acquire.

∗ Memorizing the fractional equivalents below is useful.

$$\tfrac{1}{8} = 12\tfrac{1}{2}\% \qquad\qquad \tfrac{1}{3} = 33\tfrac{1}{3}\% \qquad\qquad \tfrac{1}{6} = 16\tfrac{2}{3}\%$$

∗ Understand how $\tfrac{7}{8} = 1 - .12\tfrac{1}{2} = .87\tfrac{1}{2}$,
  and $\tfrac{5}{6} = 1 - .16\tfrac{2}{3} = .83\tfrac{1}{3}$.

Use the charts below for analyzing percents. Introduce the charts before assigning page 80 . Duplicate them on the chalkboard or on a transparency.

A	B	C
100% of 800 = 800	100% of 145 = 145	100% of 72 = 72
10% of 800 = 80	10% of 145 = 14.5	10% of 72 = 7.2
1% of 800 = 8	1% of 145 = 1.45	1% of 72 = .72

At some point, Charts B and C can be used to expand the lesson to other tens numbers. Students could make up their own percent examples; for example: 20% of 14.5 or 30% of 72.

Name _____

Analyzing 1%, 10%, and 100% of a Number

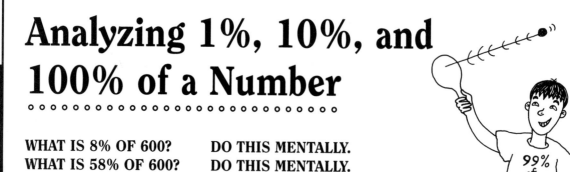

○ ○

WHAT IS 8% OF 600? **DO THIS MENTALLY.**
WHAT IS 58% OF 600? **DO THIS MENTALLY.**

Hard questions? Definitely **NOT**! These are *easy* when you know the information in the examples below. It's remarkable what you can do with basic information!

EXAMPLES:	100% of 600 = 600
	10% of 600 = 60
	1% of 600 = 6

Answer the following questions based on the information in the examples.

1. What is 100% of 600? _____   2. What is 2% of 600? _____

3. What is 50 % of 600? _____   4. What is 3% of 600? _____

5. What is 10% of 600? _____   6. What is 15% of 600? _____

7. What is 5% of 600? _____   8. What is 8% of 600? _____

9. What is 1% of 600? _____   10. What is 23 % of 600? _____

11. What is $\frac{1}{2}$% of 600? _____   12. What is 41% of 600? _____

13. What is 200% of 600? _____   14. What is 58% of 600? _____

15. What is 20% of 600? _____   16. What is $1\frac{1}{2}$% of 600? _____

17. What is 30% of 600? _____   18. What is $10\frac{1}{2}$% of 600? _____

19. What is 40% of 600? _____   20. What is $99\frac{1}{2}$% of 600? _____

21. What is 60% of 600? _____   22. What is 95% of 600? _____

At what point did you stop looking at the chart?

80

Name _____

Percents and Fraction Equivalents: A Time Saver

CHANGING FRACTIONS TO PERCENTS

✳ When written as a fraction with a denominator of 100, some percents can be renamed easily as fractions with familiar denominators such as $\frac{1}{4}$, $\frac{1}{5}$, $\frac{1}{10}$, $\frac{1}{20}$ and $\frac{1}{50}$.
Some examples are: $35\% = \frac{35}{100} = \frac{7}{20}$; $48\% = \frac{48}{100} = \frac{12}{25}$.

✳ There are three fraction/percent equivalents you need to **memorize**.

$\frac{1}{8} = 12\frac{1}{2}\%$ $\frac{1}{3} = 33\frac{1}{3}\%$ $\frac{1}{6} = 16\frac{2}{3}\%$

Mentally change the fractions below to percents. Use what you know about the unit fraction.

EXAMPLE: If you know that $\frac{1}{25} = 4\%$, then $\frac{9}{25}$ is 9 x 4 or 36%.

1. $\frac{1}{2} = $ ___%   2. $\frac{1}{4} = $ ___%   3. $\frac{1}{8} = $ ___%   4. $\frac{1}{6} = $ ___%

5. $\frac{1}{3} = $ ___%   6. $\frac{2}{4} = \frac{1}{2} = $ ___%   7. $\frac{2}{8} = \frac{1}{4} = $ ___%   8. $\frac{2}{6} = \frac{1}{3} = $ ___%

9. $\frac{2}{3} = $ ___%   10. $\frac{3}{4} = $ ___%   11. $\frac{3}{8} = $ ___%   12. $\frac{5}{6} = $ ___%

13. $\frac{1}{10} = $ ___%   14. $\frac{1}{5} = $ ___%   15. $\frac{1}{50} = $ ___%   16. $\frac{7}{25} = $ ___%

17. $\frac{2}{10} = $ ___%   18. $\frac{2}{5} = $ ___%   19. $\frac{11}{50} = $ ___%   20. $\frac{1}{20} = $ ___%

21. $\frac{8}{10} = $ ___%   22. $\frac{4}{5} = $ ___%   23. $\frac{1}{25} = $ ___%   24. $\frac{13}{20} = $ ___%

✳ Remember to think of the fraction as the percent over 100 and then put it into the best form.

✳ Remember to make use of the fraction/percent equivalents; for example: $28\% = \frac{28}{100} = \frac{7}{25}$.

Mentally change the percents to fractions.

25. 35%= _____   **26.** $66\frac{2}{3}\%$ = _____   **27.** 75% = _____   **28.** 22% = _____

29. 40%= _____   **30.** $87\frac{1}{2}\%$ = _____   **31.** 48% = _____   **32.** 12% = _____

33. 15%= _____   **34.** $83\frac{1}{3}\%$ = _____   **35.** 70% = _____   **36.** 55% = _____

37. 24%= _____   **38.** $16\frac{2}{3}\%$ = _____   **39.** 68% = _____   **40.** 8% = _____

Name _____

Using Fractional Equivalents and Role Reversal

○ ○

What is **ROLE REVERSAL**?

ROLE REVERSAL *is changing the problem around to produce an easier set of operating numbers.*

EXAMPLE: 18% of 50 can be mentally changed to 50% of 18, or $\frac{1}{2}$ of 18.

This works because 18% of 50 = $\frac{18}{100}$ x $\frac{50}{1}$, or $\frac{18}{1}$ x $\frac{50}{100}$

18 x 50% is the same as 18 x $\frac{1}{2}$ = 9.

Use fractional equivalents to do the examples below mentally . Use ROLE REVERSAL where it is helpful.

1. 50% of 400 = _____

2. 75% of 40 = _____

3. 60% of 35 = _____

4. $16\frac{2}{3}$% of \$42. = _____

5. 30% of 20 = _____

6. $33\frac{1}{3}$% x 24 = _____

7. 80% x 30 = _____

8. 12% of 75 = _____

9. 44% of 50 = _____

10. 25% of 84 = _____

11. 14% x 50 = _____

12. 55% x \$200. = _____

13. 36% x \$25. = _____

14. 65% x 100 = _____

You can use this same idea with decimals.

15. .08 x \$125. = _____

16. .60 x 80 = _____

17. .48 x 75 = _____

18. $.87\frac{1}{2}$ x 64 = _____

19. .90 x 40 = _____

20. $.37\frac{1}{2}$ x 32 = _____

Playing Percentages

DIRECTIONS: Cut out and distribute to students. A student reads his or her card. The student who has the correct number on his or her card should answer. The game continues until the first card is repeated. Substituting with fractions can be helpful.

I have

80

Who has 50% of
my number?

I have

40

Who has 25% of
my number?

I have

10

Who has 150% of
my number?

I have

15

Who has 200% of
my number?

I have

30

Who has 110% of
my number?

I have

33

Who has 200% of
my number?

I have

66

Who has 6 less than
my number?

I have

60

Who has 30% of
my number

I have

18

Who has 10 times
my number?

I have

180

Who has 50% of
my number?

I have

90

Who has 110% of
my number?

I have

99

Who has
19 less?

Begin with the worksheet **MENTALLY SQUARING SOME MULTIPLES OF 5.** Read aloud the first part of the worksheet or ask a student to do so. Be sure that the students know the three steps in the sequence.

Then ask, "How can we square 55?" Check to be sure the three steps are understood. Next try 85.

55^2	85^2
6 x 5 = 30	9 x 8 = 72
5 x 5 = 25	5 x 5 = 25
3,025	7,225

After the students have finished and checked the eight examples, ask, "If we know the square of 35 is 1,225, how can we work backwards to find the square root of 1,225?" After a discussion, read the section on finding square roots. Have the students compare their thinking with the worksheet. Encourage them to follow the strategy and then look at the previous work to check themselves.

For **MENTALLY USING EXPONENTS**, encourage students to predict the number of zeroes in 10^4, 10^6. Write 2.71×10^3 on the chalkboard. Ask, "What would you have to multiply 2.71 by in order to write the expression in standard form? (1,000) What would be the standard form for 2.71×10^3?" (2,710) Assign the worksheet after the discussion, or when you feel that students can handle all of the work independently.

For the worksheet **USING SCIENTIFIC NOTATION**, stress the meaning of scientific notation. Discuss the following:

* the requirements of scientific notation
* factors
* range of the factors
* why scientists use scientific notation.

Name _____

Mentally Squaring Some Multiples of 5

o o o o o o o o o o o o o o o o o o o o o o o o o o o o o o

What is 35^2 ?

Here is how you can square this multiple of 5 *mentally*.

* Multiply the 3 by its next higher number. $4 \times 3 = 12$

* The last two digits in the answer are 25. Why?

* Put the 12 and the 25 together. (1,225)

Square all the two-digit numbers ending in 5. Use the strategy shown above.

1. 15^2 = _____   **2.** 65^2 = _____   **3.** 25^2 = _____

4. 75^2 = _____   **5.** 45^2 = _____   **6.** 85^2 = _____

7. 55^2 = _____   **8.** 95^2 = _____   **9.** 105^2 = _____

To find the square root of numbers mentally, the strategy is to reverse the above process.

* Separate the rest of the numbers from 25. Find the $\sqrt{25}$.

* Next, determine what two consecutive factors will give the product of the remaining number. Keep the smaller factor and place it before the 5.

EXAMPLE: Find the $\sqrt{1,225}$

* The $\sqrt{25}$ is 5.

* $3 \times 4 = 12$, keep the 3. Put it before the 5 to make 35.

Mentally calculate the square root of each of the following numbers using the above strategy.

10. $\sqrt{2,025}$ = _____   **11.** $\sqrt{625}$ = _____

12. $\sqrt{225}$ = _____   **13.** $\sqrt{4,225}$ = _____

14. $\sqrt{9,025}$ = _____   **15.** $\sqrt{3,025}$ = _____

16. $\sqrt{5,625}$ = _____   **17.** $\sqrt{7,225}$ = _____

Name _____

Mentally Using Exponents

○ ○

What pattern do you see below between the exponent and the number of zeroes in the standard form of each number?

$$10^1 = 10 \qquad 10^2 = 100 \qquad 10^3 = 1,000$$

Write the standard form:

1. 10^4 = _____   **2.** 10^5 = _____

How would you write each as a power of 10?

3. 1,000,000 = _____   **4.** 100,000,000 = _____

How would you write each of the following as a product of a factor and a power of 10?

EXAMPLES: $600 = 6 \times 100 = \underline{6 \times 10^2}$ $750 = \underline{75 \times 10^1}$ $587,000 = \underline{587 \times 10^3}$

5. 6,000 = _____   **6.** 250,000 = _____

7. 86,200 = _____   **8.** 3,500 = _____

9. 32,000,000 = _____   **10.** 9,500,000 = _____

Write in standard form:

11. 42×10^5 = _____   **12.** 4×10^2 = _____

13. 4.1×10^2 = _____   **14.** 7.8×10^3 = _____

15. 2.8×10^3 = _____   **16.** 8.345×10^2 = _____

Name _____

Mental Practice with Scientific Notation

•○•○•○•○•○•○•○•○•○•○•○•○•○•○•○•○•○

SCIENTIFIC NOTATION is expressing a number as a product of a factor and a power of 10. The *factor*, however, must be between 1 and 10.

EXAMPLES: $23{,}000 = 2.3 \times 10^4$ $5{,}670 = 5.67 \times 10^3$ $24.5 = 2.45 \times 10^1$

Write in standard form.

1. $1.68 \times 10^3 =$ _____

2. $5 \times 10^4 =$ _____

3. $2.137 \times 10^2 =$ _____

4. $3.06 \times 10^2 =$ _____

5. $2.13 \times 10^4 =$ _____

6. $9.9 \times 10^5 =$ _____

7. $8 \times 10^3 =$ _____

8. $6.15 \times 10^1 =$ _____

9. $4.03 \times 10^1 =$ _____

10. $2.4 \times 10^4 =$ _____

11. $8.013 \times 10^1 =$ _____

12. $5.1 \times 10^3 =$ _____

Write each in scientific notation.

13. $580 =$ _____

14. $47.8 =$ _____

15. $360{,}000 =$ _____

16. $248 =$ _____

17. $347 =$ _____

18. $692.5 =$ _____

19. $9{,}600 =$ _____

20. $24.8 =$ _____

21. $21.8 =$ _____

22. $17.1 =$ _____

23. $7{,}250 =$ _____

24. $4{,}600 =$ _____

25. $4{,}000 =$ _____

26. $7{,}200 =$ _____

27. $200{,}000 =$ _____

28. $3{,}000 =$ _____

ANSWER KEY

PAGE 12
1. 6,358
$731,217
2. 267,762
432,140
3. 21,400
134,000
4. 30,000
10,000
5. 1,225
9,025
6. 8,991
69,993
7. 14
.000167
8. 85
55
9. N = 15
N = 36
10. 90
11. 9

PAGE 14
1. 768 miles
2. 12 lawns
3. 1½ cups
4. 6 x (7.98 + .02);
6 x 8 = 48;
48 - (6 x .02);
48 - (.12); 47.88
5. $1.00
6. 3 bags
7. $20.00
8. 4/$23.00

PAGE 15
1. 13, 100, 23, 101,
1,000
2. 18, 33, 95, 101,
113
3. 33, 106, 122,
224, 406
4. 36, 52, 67, 102,
125, 216, 447,
688
5. 97, 40, 102, 168,
256
6. 121, 336, 846,
1,023, 864
7. 138, 390, 972,
824, 2,443
8. 134, 267, 372,
297, 555, 598,
632, 885

PAGE 16
1. 8, 10, 12, 14, 16,
18, 20, 22, 24, 26
2. 12, 15, 18, 21,
24, 27, 30, 33,
36, 39
3. 20, 25, 30, 35,
40, 45, 50, 55,
60, 65
4. 40, 50, 60, 70,
80, 90, 100, 110,
120, 130
5. 80, 100, 120,
140, 160, 180,
200, 220, 240,
260
6. 100, 125, 150,
175, 200, 225,
250, 275, 300,
325
7. 200, 250, 300,
350, 400, 450,
500, 550, 600,
650
8. 400; 500; 600;
700; 800; 900;
1,000; 1,100;
1,200; 1,300
9. 396; 495; 594;
693; 792; 891;
900; 1,089;
1,188; 1,287
10. 332; 432; 532;
632; 732; 832;
932; 1,032;
1,132; 1,232

PAGE 17
1. 6, 99, 200, 549,
776
2. 990, 197, 298,
554, 638
3. 23, 231, 506,
798, 990
4. 78, 15, 22, 31, 89
5. 282; 391; 605;
899; 1,011
6. 14, 31, 52, 66, 94
7. 268, 401, 329,
263, 46
8. 63, 101, 95, 524,
296

PAGE 18
1. 84, 82, 80, 78,
76, 74, 72, 70,
68, 66
2. 51, 48, 45, 42,
39, 36, 33, 30,
27, 24
3. 105, 100, 95, 90,
85, 80, 75, 70,
65, 60
4. 140, 130, 120,
110, 100, 90, 80,
70, 60, 50
5. 340, 320, 300,
280, 260, 240,
220, 200, 180,
160
6. 250, 225, 200,
175, 150, 125,
100, 75, 50, 25
7. 650, 600, 550,
500, 450, 400,
350, 300, 250,
200
8. 1,700; 1,600;
1,500; 1,400;
1,300; 1,200;
1,100; 1,000;
900; 800
9. 990, 891, 792,
693, 594, 495,
396, 297, 198, 99
10. 313, 303, 293,
283, 273, 263,
253, 243, 233,
223

PAGE 20
column one: 28, 38,
48, 58, 68, 78,
88, 98
column two: 13, 23,
33, 43, 53, 63,
73, 83, 93
column three: 16, 26,
36, 46, 56, 66,
76, 86, 96
column four: 19, 29,
39, 49, 59, 69,
79, 89, 99
column five: 17, 27,
37, 47, 57, 67,
77, 87, 97

PAGE 21
1. 36
2. 55
3. 37
4. 25
5. 53
6. 35
7. 97
8. 25
9. 15
10. 40
11. 37
12. 78
13. 43
14. 25
15. 98
16. 21
17. 35
18. 47
19. 38
20. 24

PAGE 22
1. 33, 35, 55, 53
2. 14, 16, 36, 34
3. 28, 30, 50, 48
4. 64, 66, 86, 84
5. 75, 77, 97, 95
6. 11, 13, 33, 31
7. 42, 44, 64, 62
8. 50, 52, 72, 70
9. 37, 39, 59, 57
10. 4, 6, 26, 24
11. 48, 50, 70, 68
12. 71, 73, 93, 91

PAGE 28
1. 72
2. 41
3. 121
4. 92
5. 41
6. 62
7. 71
8. 41

PAGE 29
1. 62, 43, 51, 44,
83, 94, 74, 55, 41
2. 94, 37, 51, 28,
82, 78, 43, 91, 48
3. 81, 23, 34, 82,
71, 54, 41, 92, 24
4. 25, 31, 44, 96,

81, 63, 92, 83, 52
5. 22, 63, 81, 23,
   41, 92, 53, 91, 83
6. 82, 51, 86, 76,
   65, 43, 34, 63, 96
7. 41, 21, 62, 92,
   42, 31, 22, 81, 72

PAGE 31
1. 64
2. 54
3. 57
4. 51
5. 57
6. 62
7. 44
8. 92
9. 97
10. 87
11. 61
12. 53
13. 117
14. 82
15. 97
16. 63
17. 61
18. 127
19. 94
20. 96
21. 110
22. 163
23. 183
24. 252
25. 185
26. 139
27. 95
28. 141
29. 291
30. 628

PAGE 32
1. 772
2. 1,388
3. $5.43
4. 334
5. 2,777
6. 474
7. 555
8. 5,678
9. 324
10. 1,022
11. 820
12. 8,845
13. 494
14. 6,884
15. 527
16. 197
17. 336

18. 113
19. 861
20. 558
21. 1,024
22. 786
23. 231
24. 643
25. 921
26. 3,488

PAGE 33
1. 30
2. 13 + 75
3. 20
4. 30 + 80
5. 70
6. 70 + 82
7. 70 + 30, or
   80 + 20, or
   25 + 75
8. 31 + 70
9. 80
10. 25 + 82
11. 13 + 25
12. 30 + 82
13. 20
14. 69 + 82
15. 75
16. 70 + 80
17. 31 + 82
18. 22 + 70
19. 22 + 82
20. 69 + 80

PAGE 34
Strategy 1
1. 24
2. 43
3. 25
4. 34
5. 33
6. 19
Strategy 2
1. 75
2. 25
3. 166
4. 18
5. 23
6. 146
Strategy 3
1. 22
2. 29
3. 66
4. 16
5. 147
6. 160

PAGE 35
Subtracting Nice
Numbers
1. 664
2. 120
3. 479
4. 235
5. 656
6. 848
7. 754
8. 187
9. 420
10. 494
11. 579
12. 505
13. 526
14. 159
15. 70
16. 583
17. 194
18. 163
19. 391
20. 557
21. 4,476
22. 7,432
Subtracting Nicer
Numbers
1. 325
2. 293
3. 134
4. 511
5. 659
6. 356
7. 822
8. 582
9. 25
10. 434
11. 711
12. 1,486

PAGE 36
Examples
68; 528; 3,747;
42,866; 743,753
1. 62
2. 14
3. 38
4. 66
5. 45
6. 57
7. 538
8. 153
9. 399
10. 662
11. 4,868
12. 1,649
13. 7,652
14. 11,614

15. 74,236
16. 532,108
17. 154,375
18. 267,439
19. 795,433
20. 6,600

PAGE 37
1. 80 - 70, or 30 -20
2. 70 - 25
3. 70 - 20, or 80 -
   30
4. 25
5. 30
6. 75
7. 25 - 22
8. 70 - 30
9. 75
10. 30 - 22
11. 13
12. 31 - 20
13. 20 - 13
14. 80
15. 75 - 31
16. 69
17. 31
18. 80 - 25, or
   75 - 20
19. 80 - 20
20. 31

PAGE 38
1. 352
2. 748
3. 33,781
4. 4,675
5. 3,949
6. 46,068
7. 39,886
8. 31,625
9. 108,636
10. 7,958,764
11. 260,238
12. 382,877

PAGE 39
Examples
70; 4,000; 100,000
1. 6,300
2. 2,000
3. 1,800
4. 5,600
5. 750
6. 18,000
7. 36,000
8. 35,000
9. 48,000
10. 3,600

11. 120,000
12. 4,500,000
13. 100,000
14. 30,000
15. 36,000
16. 240,000
17. 32,000
18. 3,000
19. 10,000
20. 70,000

PAGE 40

1. 2,220
2. 4,300
3. 32,000
4. 3,120
5. 1,200
6. 21,000
7. 4,320
8. 1,800
9. 406,000
10. 760
11. 2,400
12. 36,000
13. 675
14. 1,350
15. 9,500
16. 4,050

PAGE 41

1. 495
2. 3,996
3. 216
4. 35,964
5. 1,584
6. 11,988

PAGE 42

Top of Page
1. $11.70
2. 1,140
3. 2,392
4. 885
5. $89.55
6. 1,188
7. $23.80
8. $49.75
9. 3,594
Bottom of Page
1. 600
2. 3,200
3. 2,800
4. 540
5. 256
6. 900
7. 280
8. 2,300
9. 1,000

10. 260
11. 360
12. 450
13. 200
14. 6,000
15. 210
16. 72
17. 1,200
18. 1,800

PAGE 43

1. 10 x 69
2. 30 x 22
3. 20 x 30
4. 70 x 30
5. 80 x 70
6. 10 x 22
7. 20 x 80
8. 11 x 82
9. 11 x 22
10. 20 x 25
11. 13 x 20
12. 10 x 82
13. 31 x 20
14. 13 x 30
15. 11 x 25
16. 69 x 11
17. 25 x 30, or
    10 x 75
18. 11 x 80
19. 70 x 20
20. 10 x 30

PAGE 44

Step 1: 10 ÷ 5; $9\overline{)36}$

Step 2: $9\overline{)16}$ R 7;
$7\overline{)48}$ R 6
Box I: 1,2,1,3,4,4
    3,2,6,7,0,1
Box II: 2,1,3,4,1,2
    4,3,0,4,6,2
Box III: 5,7,5,1,1,6
    0,6,7,8,0,4
1. 1
2. 0
3. 0
4. 4
5. 1
6. 1
7. 4
8. 0
9. 0
10. 6
11. 0
12. 6
13. 3
14. 0

15. 1
16. 3
17. 2
18. 4
19. 1
20. 3
21. 4

PAGE 45

Top of Page
1. 124
2. 30
3. 50
4. 111
5. 241
6. 81
7. 41
8. 41
9. 71
10. 60
11. 91
12. 421
13. 51
14. 50
15. 70
16. 80
17. 321
18. 100
19. 54
20. 71
21. 92
22. 321
23. 111
24. 81
25. 121
26. 213
27. 81
28. 204
29. 123
30. 43
Bottom of Page
1. F
2. H
3. G
4. A
5. D
6. J
7. E
8. I
9. B
10. C
11. I
12. F
13. B
14. J
15. C
16. H
17. G

18. A
19. E
20. D

PAGE 46

What is 2?
1. $40\overline{)80}$
2. $60\overline{)120}$
3. $4\overline{)8}$

What is 3?
1. $40\overline{)120}$
2. 210 ÷ 70
3. $90\overline{)270}$

What is 4?
1. 320 ÷ 80
2. $3\overline{)12}$
3. 120 ÷ 30

What is 5?
2. 35 ÷ 7
3. $8\overline{)40}$

What is 6?
1. $90\overline{)540}$
2. 240 ÷ 40
3. $7\overline{)42}$

What is 7?
1. 490 ÷ 70
2. 280 ÷ 40
3. 350 ÷ 50

What is 8?
1. $90\overline{)720}$
2. $60\overline{)480}$
3. 240 ÷ 30

What is 9?
1. 450 ÷ 50
2. 36 ÷ 4
3. 63 ÷ 7

PAGE 47

1. 9
2. 70 ÷ 5
3. 5
4. 70 = 60, or

$60 = 70$
5. 40
6. $80 \div 40$
7. 5
8. 3
9. 60
10. 7
11. 5
12. $40 \div 8$
13. 60
14. 8
15. 80
16. $70 \div 7$
17. 40
18. 60
19. 60
20. 3

PAGE 50
1. 2, 3, 4, 8
2. 2, 4, 2, 4
3. 2, 2, 6, 10
4. 2, 2, 6, 12
5. 1, 2, 2, 6
6. 12, 6, 2, 4
7. 4, 2, 1, 10

PAGE 51
1. $1\frac{1}{3}$
2. $1\frac{3}{4}$
3. $1\frac{3}{8}$
4. $1\frac{2}{3}$
5. $1\frac{1}{8}$
6. 2
7. 2
8. 2
9. $2\frac{1}{4}$
10. $2\frac{1}{3}$
11. $2\frac{1}{6}$

PAGE 52
1. $\frac{5}{8} + \frac{3}{8}$
2. $\frac{1}{4} + \frac{3}{4}$
3. $\frac{1}{2} + \frac{1}{2}$
4. $\frac{1}{6} + \frac{2}{6} + \frac{3}{6}$
5. $\frac{2}{3} + \frac{1}{3}$
6. $\frac{3}{5} + \frac{1}{5} + \frac{1}{5}$
7. $\frac{3}{6} + \frac{4}{8}$
8. $\frac{2}{5} + \frac{6}{10}$
9. $\frac{6}{12} + \frac{5}{10}$
10. $\frac{5}{10} + \frac{1}{2}$
11. $\frac{6}{8} + \frac{1}{4}$
12. $\frac{1}{3} + \frac{4}{6}$
13. $\frac{4}{10} + \frac{3}{5}$
14. $\frac{9}{12} + \frac{2}{8}$
15. $\frac{8}{16} + \frac{1}{2}$
16. $\frac{2}{6} + \frac{2}{3}$

17. $\frac{8}{12} + \frac{2}{6}$
18. $\frac{8}{12} + \frac{1}{3}$

PAGE 53
1. $\frac{3}{4}$
2. $\frac{5}{6}$
3. $\frac{7}{8}$
4. $\frac{9}{10}$
5. $\frac{5}{6}$
6. $1\frac{1}{6}$
7. $1\frac{1}{12}$
8. $1\frac{3}{8}$
9. $\frac{5}{6}$
10. $1\frac{1}{6}$
11. $1\frac{1}{12}$
12. $1\frac{3}{8}$
13. $1\frac{1}{3}$
14. $1\frac{2}{3}$
15. $4\frac{2}{5}$
16. $6\frac{1}{2}$
17. $6\frac{3}{8}$
18. $1\frac{1}{4}$
19. $1\frac{7}{8}$
20. $1\frac{1}{4}$
21. $5\frac{4}{5}$
22. $10\frac{7}{10}$
23. 2
24. $8\frac{1}{2}$

PAGE 54
1. $1\frac{1}{6}$
2. $9\frac{1}{2}$
3. $8\frac{3}{8}$
4. $9\frac{1}{5}$
5. $5\frac{1}{4}$
6. $5\frac{1}{3}$
7. $6\frac{4}{5}$
8. $5\frac{1}{2}$
9. $11\frac{1}{8}$
10. $10\frac{3}{10}$
11. $8\frac{1}{2}$
12. 6
13. $7\frac{5}{8}$
14. $9\frac{7}{8}$
15. $9\frac{11}{12}$
16. $4\frac{3}{4}$

PAGE 55
1. $\frac{1}{4}$
2. $\frac{3}{5}$
3. $\frac{2}{5}$
4. $\frac{2}{3}$
5. $\frac{1}{3}$
6. $\frac{3}{8}$
7. $\frac{2}{5}$
8. $\frac{5}{12}$
9. $\frac{7}{16}$
10. $1\frac{3}{4}$

11. $4\frac{1}{4}$
12. $2\frac{1}{8}$
13. $5\frac{1}{5}$
14. $1\frac{7}{16}$
15. $4\frac{1}{5}$
16. $3\frac{1}{3}$
17. $2\frac{1}{4}$
18. $4\frac{1}{3}$
19. $1\frac{4}{5}$
20. $2\frac{5}{8}$
21. $4\frac{1}{5}$
22. $4\frac{2}{5}$
23. $\frac{1}{4}$
24. $1\frac{1}{3}$
25. $1\frac{3}{4}$
26. $1\frac{1}{3}$
27. $1\frac{1}{6}$

PAGE 56
1. 4
2. 8
3. 3
4. 12
5. 16
6. 5
7. 6
8. 10
9. 5
10. 5
11. 8
12. 14
13. 8
14. 10
15. 13
16. 28
17. $2\frac{3}{4}$
18. $4\frac{5}{6}$
19. $6\frac{3}{5}$
20. $1\frac{4}{8}$
21. $7\frac{1}{2}$
22. $\frac{4}{5}$
23. $3\frac{4}{5}$
24. $2\frac{5}{6}$
25. $6\frac{2}{3}$
26. $5\frac{3}{4}$
27. $\frac{3}{5}$
28. $1\frac{2}{3}$
29. $3\frac{3}{10}$
30. $6\frac{2}{3}$
31. $2\frac{3}{4}$
32. $6\frac{5}{6}$
33. $4\frac{5}{6}$
34. $\frac{3}{5}$
35. $4\frac{3}{4}$
36. $2\frac{4}{5}$
37. $1\frac{5}{8}$
38. $1\frac{3}{5}$
39. $2\frac{7}{8}$

40. $2\frac{4}{5}$

PAGE 57
1. 2
2. 4
3. 3
4. 6
5. 2
6. 4
7. 6
8. 3
9. 8
10. 9
11. 4
12. 12
13. $\frac{1}{4}$
14. $\frac{1}{3}$
15. $\frac{1}{4}$
16. $\frac{1}{4}$
17. $\frac{1}{12}$
18. $\frac{1}{5}$
19. $\frac{1}{12}$
20. $\frac{1}{8}$
21. $\frac{1}{8}$
22. $\frac{5}{12}$
23. $\frac{1}{10}$
24. $\frac{1}{4}$
25. $\frac{1}{12}$
26. $\frac{3}{16}$
27. $\frac{7}{10}$
28. $\frac{3}{16}$
29. $\frac{1}{6}$
30. $3\frac{1}{8}$
31. $2\frac{1}{4}$
32. $7\frac{1}{4}$
33. 4
34. $5\frac{1}{8}$
35. $4\frac{1}{5}$
36. $6\frac{1}{4}$
37. $1\frac{1}{6}$
38. $\frac{2}{5}$
39. $2\frac{1}{6}$
40. $5\frac{1}{8}$
41. $2\frac{1}{4}$
42. $6\frac{1}{2}$

PAGE 58
1. 2
2. 5
3. 7
4. 9
5. 10
6. 14
7. 16
8. 19
9. 20
10. 24
11. 30¢

92

12. 45¢
13. $ .50
14. 150
15. 250
16. 400
17. 600
18. 740
19. 1,319
20. 1.24
21. 8.014
22. 15
23. 35
24. 45
25. 65
26. 75
27. $12\frac{1}{2}$
28. $37\frac{1}{2}$
29. $41\frac{1}{2}$
30. $49\frac{1}{2}$
31. $\frac{1}{4}$
32. $\frac{1}{16}$
33. $\frac{1}{6}$
34. $\frac{1}{3}$
35. $\frac{1}{10}$
36. $\frac{1}{7}$
37. $2\frac{1}{6}$
38. $3\frac{1}{6}$
39. $5\frac{1}{8}$
40. $7\frac{3}{4}$
41. 8
42. .30
43. 10
44. .40
45. 15
46. .50
47. 20
48. .60
49. 25¢
50. 7.5
51. 5
52. .50
53. 15
54. .60
55. 20
56. 1.00
57. 25
58. 11.1
59. 30
60. 1.20
61. .7
62. 2.5
63. 1.0
64. .51
65. 1.1
66. .62
67. 1.5
68. 11.1
69. 20

70. 1.21

PAGE 59
1. 4
2. 9
3. 15
4. 4
5. 18
6. 24
7. 4
8. 21
9. 20
10. 20
11. 12
12. 12
13. 35
14. 22
15. 30
16. 10
17. 35
18. 6
19. 8
20. 21
21. 48
22. 50
23. 150
24. 210
25. 350
26. 20
27. 63
28. 33
29. 16
30. 30

PAGE 60
1. 2
2. 6
3. 4
4. 5
5. 15
6. 8
7. 3
8. 3
9. 2
10. 3
11. 75
12. 5
13. 32
14. 3
15. 51
16. 20
17. 3
18. 33
19. 3
20. 49
21. 16
22. 3
23. 10

24. 45
25. 1
26. 60
27. 8
28. 65

PAGE 62
1. 2
2. 2
3. 5
4. 6
5. 7
6. 6
7. 14
8. 1
9. 2
10. 3
11. 2
12. 2
13. 3
14. 2
15. 2
16. 4
17. 4
18. 4
19. 5
20. 2
21. 7
22. 2
23. 2
24. 4
25. 6
26. 4
27. 8
28. 12
29. 8
30. 12
31. 40
32. 20
33. 8
34. 3
35. 10
36. 18
37. 24
38. 35
39. 48
40. 20
41. 3
42. 7
43. 5
44. 9
45. 17
46. 14
47. 7
48. 3
49. 8
50. 5
51. 7

52. 9
53. 36
54. 23

PAGE 64
1. 2
2. 2
3. 1
4. 1
5. 2
6. 1
7. 3
8. 5
9. 3
10. 4
11. 1
12. 2
13. 3
14. 4
15. 4
16. 3
17. 1
18. 3
19. 2
20. 1
21. 6
22. 14
23. 15
24. 18
25. 17
26. 26
27. 23
28. 8
29. 2
30. 16
31. 11
32. 38
33. 13

PAGE 66
1. 8.4, 5.3, 1.9,
   2.8, 4.0, 16.7,
   39.4, 2.6
2. 63.6, 92.2, 21.0,
   26.9, 86.4, 45.5,
   23.6, 71.7
3. .97, 3.20, 3.64,
   8.124, 5.734,
   5.215, 10.342,
   .67
4. 1.14, 6.93, 3.65,
   5.530, 9.175,
   3.321, 10.457,
   1.05

PAGE 67
1. .5, .8, 1.1, 1.4,
   1.7

93

2. 1.7, 2.1, 2.5, 2.9, 3.3
3. 1.9, 2.4, 2.9, 3.4, 3.9
4. 4.0, 4.6, 5.2, 5.8, 6.4
5. 6.5, 7.2, 7.9, 8.6, 9.3
6. 5.1, 5.9, 6.7, 7.5, 8.3
7. 3.0, 3.9, 4.8, 5.7, 6.6

PAGE 68
1. .55, .663, 2.745, 5.6, 8.063
2. .393, 6.2097, 5.3587, 2.941, 2.462
3. .673, 9.768, 3.3263, 8.4543, .7353
4. 2.972, 7.771, 4.838, 2.402, .6903
5. .096, 1.13, 2.201, 4.673, 10.011
6. 3.166, .4335, 6.417, 3.3646, 1.7371

PAGE 69
1. 6.7, 6.4, 6.1, 5.8, 5.5, 5.2, 4.9, 4.6, 4.3, 4.0, 3.7
2. 4.3, 3.9, 3.5, 3.1, 2.7, 2.3, 1.9, 1.5, 1.1, 0.7, 0.3
3. 8.8, 8.3, 7.8, 7.3, 6.8, 6.3, 5.8, 5.3, 4.8, 4.3, 3.8
4. 8.1, 7.5, 6.9, 6.3, 5.7, 5.1, 4.5, 3.9, 3.3, 2.7, 2.1
5. 14.6, 13.9, 13.2, 12.5, 11.8, 11.1, 10.4, 9.7, 9.0, 8.3, 7.6
6. 19.7, 18.9, 18.1, 17.3, 16.5, 15.7, 14.9, 14.1, 13.3, 12.5, 11.7
7. 18.2, 17.3, 16.4, 15.5, 14.6. 13.7, 12.8, 11.9, 11.0, 10.1, 9.2

PAGE 70
1. 3.25, 4.50, 4.75, 6.00, 4.10, 3.15
2. 4.50, 3.75, 3.25, 6.0, 6.50, 6.10, 4.30, 3.15
3. 8.50, 2.50, 1.50, 1.25, 2.75, 4.00, .10, 1.30
4. .25, 1.25, 3.00, 2.75, .50, 6.05, 3.15, 2.11

PAGE 71
Examples: .524, 3.427, 3.713, .5317, 65.32108
1. .62
2. .174
3. .649
4. 5.3
5. 4.87
6. 7.076
7. 3.5676
8. 62.5722
9. 6.2755
10. 23.55179
11. 2.640
12. .4390
13. 16.60
14. 380.0

PAGE 72
For: .25
　.75 - .50
　.50 - .25
For: .50
　.75 - .25
　1.25 - .75
　1.75 - 1.25
　3.00 - 2.50
For: 1.00
　1.25 - .25
　1.75 - .75
For: 1.25
　1.75 - .50
　2.50 -1.25
　3.00 - 1.75
　4.25 - 3.00
For: 2.00
　2.50 - .50
For: 3.00
　4.25 - 1.25
For: 4.00
　4.25 - .25

PAGE 73
1. 10

2. 10
3. 1,000
4. 10
5. 100
6. 10
7. 100
8. 100
9. 10
10. 1,000
11. 100
12. 10
13. 32.4
14. 45
15. 67
16. 5,120
17. 399,700
18. 621
19. .08
20. 921
21. 762.15
22. 98,300
23. 456.3
24. 9.114
25. .1
26. .110
27. 14.47
28. 100
29. 43
30. 45

PAGE 74
1. .7
2. .09
3. .09
4. .25
5. .025
6. .0023
7. .00023
8. .00415
9. .415
10. 4.15
11. .01
12. .001
13. .0001
14. .00001
15. .000001
16. .000035
17. .00006
18. .00023
19. .0008
20. .00010
21. .000006
22. .0000042
23. .0090
24. .0975

PAGE 76
1. 36.4

2. 3.64
3. .364
4. 2.548
5. .2548
6. .02548
7. .185
8. .464
9. .00513
10. .05
11. .0433
12. $ .11
13. .0126
14. .0837
15. $1.28
16. 8.634
17. 48.97
18. .5568
19. $28.67
20. .89
21. $9.86
22. .098
23. $9.60
24. .0025

PAGE 77
1. 18.4
2. 184
3. 1,840
4. 347
5. 3,470
6. 34,700
7. 4,580
8. 45,800
9. 458,000
10. 360
11. 480
12. 3,672
13. 8,840
14. 96
15. 230
16. 45
17. 78
18. 246
19. 3,420
20. 5
21. 4
22. 36
23. 1,410
24. 60

PAGE 78
1. .9
2. .06
3. .060
4. .007
5. 2.011
6. 1.002
7. 2.0006

8. .28
9. .005
10. .2
11. .08
12. .008
13. .201
14. .3
15. 3
16. .3
17. 3
18. 4
19. 40
20. .4
21. 7
22. .7
23. 8
24. 50
25. 6
26. .02
27. .101
28. 2
29. 20
30. 2

PAGE 80

1. 600
2. 12
3. 300
4. 18
5. 60
6. 90
7. 30
8. 48
9. 6
10. 138
11. 3
12. 246
13. 1,200
14. 348
15. 120
16. 9
17. 180
18. 63
19. 240
20. 597

21. 360
22. 570

PAGE 81

1. 50
2. 25
3. $12\frac{1}{2}$
4. $16\frac{2}{3}$
5. $33\frac{1}{3}$
6. 50
7. 25
8. $33\frac{1}{3}$
9. $66\frac{2}{3}$
10. 75
11. $37\frac{1}{2}$
12. $83\frac{1}{3}$
13. 10
14. 20
15. 2
16. 28
17. 20
18. 40
19. 22
20. 5
21. 80
22. 80
23. 4
24. 65
25. $\frac{7}{20}$
26. $\frac{2}{3}$
27. $\frac{3}{4}$
28. $\frac{11}{50}$
29. $\frac{2}{5}$
30. $\frac{7}{8}$
31. $\frac{12}{25}$
32. $\frac{3}{25}$
33. $\frac{3}{20}$
34. $\frac{5}{6}$
35. $\frac{7}{10}$
36. $\frac{11}{20}$
37. $\frac{6}{25}$
38. $\frac{1}{6}$
39. $\frac{17}{25}$
40. $\frac{2}{25}$

PAGE 82

1. 200
2. 30
3. 21
4. $7
5. 6
6. 8
7. 24
8. 9
9. 22
10. 21
11. 7
12. $110
13. $9
14. 65
15. $10.00
16. 48
17. 36
18. 56
19. 36
20. 12

PAGE 86

1. 225
2. 4,225
3. 625
4. 5,625
5. 2,025
6. 7,225
7. 3,025
8. 9,025
9. 11,025
10. 45
11. 25
12. 15
13. 65
14. 95
15. 55
16. 75
17. 85

PAGE 87

1. 10,000
2. 100,000
3. 10^6

4. 10^8
5. 6×10^3
5. 25×10^4
7. 862×10^2
8. 35×10^2
9. 32×10^6
10. 95×10^5
11. 4,200,000
12. 400
13. 410
14. 7,800
15. 2,800
16. 834.5

PAGE 88

1. 1,680
2. 50,000
3. 213.7
4. 306
5. 21,300
6. 990,000
7. 8,000
8. 61.5
9. 40.3
10. 24,000
11. 80.13
12. 5,100
13. 5.8×10^2
14. 4.78×10^1
15. 3.6×10^5
16. 2.48×10^2
17. 3.47×10^2
18. 6.925×10^2
19. 9.6×10^3
20. 2.48×10^1
21. 2.18×10^1
22. 1.71×10^1
23. 7.25×10^3
24. 4.6×10^3
25. 4×10^3
26. 7.2×10^3
27. 2×10^5
28. 3×10^3